"At last a much needed narrative on prolonged sobriety. Dr. Earle's story superbly demonstrates that full recovery from addictive disease includes fully rejoining, and enriching, the human race."

> James R. Milam, Ph.D.
> Professional Consultant
> Addiction Recovery Center
> Seattle

"Fascinating reading for anybody, particularly those interested in addictive disease and the long-term recovery process of the spiritual Program of Alcoholics Anonymous."

> David E. Smith, M.D.
> Founder, Medical Director of
> Haight Ashbury Free Medical Clinics
> San Francisco

"Dr. Earle portrays sobriety in the most inspired, real, and honest manner that I have ever read...this book is a gem."

> Barbara J. Stern
> Division Director, Merritt Peralta Institute
> Chemical Dependency Recovery Hospital
> Oakland, California

"I have read and reread *Physician, Heal Thyself!* and in these readings each time I see a new vista of sobriety."

> G. Douglas Talbott, M.D.
> Director, Talbott Recovery Systems
> Atlanta

Physician, Heal Thyself!

Dr. Earle M.

CompCare Publishers

Minneapolis, Minnesota

M., Earle.
    Physician, heal thyself!

    1. M., Earle. 2. Alcoholics—United States—Biography.
3. Physicians—United States—Biography. 4. Alcoholics Anonymous.
5. Alcoholics—Rehabilitation—United States. I. Title.
HV5293.M15A3 1988   362.2' 928   [B]   88-25691
ISBN 0-89638-152-8

Cover design by MacLean & Tuminelly

Interior design by Pamela Arnold

Inquiries, orders, and catalog requests should be addressed to
CompCare Publishers
2415 Annapolis Lane
Minneapolis, Minnesota 55441
Call toll free 800/328-3330
(Minnesota residents 612/559-4800)

5   4   3   2   1
93 92 91 90 89

To my wife, Mickey,
"The Little Giant"

The opinions in this book are those of the author only
and not of Alcoholics Anonymous.

CONTENTS

INFATUATION WITH AA

IRRITABILITY IN AA

INVENTIVENESS IN AA

INSIGHT IN AA

Foreword

Earle M., a very special man, has affected my life in many different ways. My earliest memory of him was in the early 1960s, when I was a medical student at the University of California at San Francisco. Earle was a prominent professor of obstetrics and gynecology, and an outstanding clinician. He was remarkable at imparting empathy for his patients to young medical students like me; the obstetrical service was one of the first places where we could practice real medicine.

How could any medical student forget Earle, standing over a model of a pelvis to demonstrate delivering babies, and saying: "Remember, men, to you having a baby would be like having a bowel movement with a football." This generated plenty of sympathy for any woman in childbirth!

Another vivid early memory was Earle's spellbinding lecture on alcoholism. In addition to my medical school work, I was studying psychopharmacology. Earle presented alcoholism as a recovering alcoholic, and he described Alcoholics Anonymous. I had never seen a recovering person before, much less a recovering physician, and AA was a totally new concept to me.

Earle was also a spiritual teacher for me. In the late 1960s I became fascinated by the relationship between psychedelic drugs and the spiritual experience, expressed by the philosophy "turn on, tune in, and drop out." Much early psychedelic drug-taking revolved around the Haight Ashbury flower children's desires to reprogram their minds. They wanted to "make love, not war," and thus to develop an alternative value system and a new society.

Although this seems naive in retrospect, at the time it dominated consciousness exploration at the Haight Ashbury, where I had started the Haight Ashbury Free Medical Clinic.

We studied all aspects of LSD in depth. We organized a conference on psychedelic drugs and religion. We invited many speakers on LSD, including Timothy Leary, the high priest of the psychedelic counterculture. Eager to include a speech on how to turn on without drugs, I remembered Earle.

The other speakers were quite interesting, but Earle carried the day. The conference was at the University of California-San Francisco, where both Earle and I were on the clinical faculty. Earle ended the day with a fascinating presentation on how to turn on with spiritual and artistic experiences instead of drugs. This culminated in a demonstration where he persuaded 800 people—half longhaired hippies from Haight Ashbury, and half health professionals from around the San Francisco Bay area—to get up on their seats and into the aisles, dancing and singing. Timothy Leary scratched his head, seemingly in dismay, as Earle stole the show. Some faculty peered into the auditorium and expressed similar dismay. Interestingly enough, there was surprisingly little complaint from UC about this most unusual conference. I guess that's what they expected when the Haight Ashbury Free Clinic put on a conference! Little did those at the medical center know that a drug-free professor excited the audience the most.

Earle has influenced my life in other ways. With a growing medical specialty of addictionology, based on the study and treatment of addictive disease, I find increasing belief by others in a better case for addictive physiology than for addictive psychology. Earle was one of the earliest to theorize that medically determined alteration in brain chemistry is responsible for the pathological response to alcoholism. Since then, researchers have defined this "x-factor"—this altered biochemical process—in some detail.

Earle also has long been a strong advocate of cross-addiction theory. He predicted that over time we may see the evolution of an "Addictions Anonymous." The trend in younger people is toward cross-addiction, and many of the newer Twelve Step programs such as Narcotics Anonymous and Cocaine Anonymous have been patterned after AA. As an old-timer in AA, Earle has tried to help open the door at the meetings he attends for cross-addicted individuals to participate in a Twelve Step process that may, in the long run, save their lives.

I read Earle's book with great fascination. I've met his daughter Jane: spent an engrossing evening discussing both opera and her father. I've also met three of Earle's wives. I'm very close to Mickey, his present wife. I work with Mickey at Merritt Peralta. Not only has Mickey made major contributions in the field of alcoholism and recovery, but also she helped my wife Millicent and me through the eighteen-hour labor of our son Christopher's birth, and she is his godmother.

This book covers Earle's interesting, diverse, and complicated life and his many world travels.

For those who are involved in the Twelve Step recovery process and who, like me, are continually trying to understand it better, this book will be an absorbing guide. Earle has long been my consultant regarding AA. When I was invited to speak as a non-alcoholic physician at AA's fiftieth anniversary in Montreal, I spent a great deal of time preparing my presentation on AA as a community resource. I checked each main point with Earle, to be sure that my interpretations were correct. So many others have depended on Earle in this capacity: as an old-timer in AA who is also modern and contemporary in thought.

Some readers might interpret this book as being critical of AA, even though Earle states over and over that AA is the best and most effective long-term route to recovery. It is critical that the Program adapt to the changing times and that there be forums for healthy discussion and interpretation. Earle provides us with this forum in his book.

Finally, I believe the most valuable aspect of this book will be the author as a role model for long-term recovery. These days, increasing numbers of people are recovering from alcoholism. But, once through the initial stages, many fail to grasp the fact that recovery is an evolving and dynamic process. Earle's experiences should help anyone in AA define the various stages and pitfalls of ongoing recovery.

I'm indebted to Earle for his many contributions to my life. His book should fascinate any reader, and particularly anyone interested in addictive disease and the long-term recovery process in the spiritual program of Alcoholics Anonymous.

David E. Smith, M.D.
Founder and Medical Director
Haight Ashbury Free Medical Clinic
San Francisco, California

Research Director
Merritt Peralta Chemical Dependence
Recovery Hospital
Oakland, California

Physician, Heal Thyself!

"I am a physician, licensed to practice in a western state. I am also an alcoholic. In two ways I may be a little different from other alcoholics. First, we all hear at AA meetings about those who have lost everything, those who have been in jail, those who have been in prison, those who have lost their families, those who have lost their income. I never lost any of it. I never was on skid row. I made more money the last year of my drinking than I ever made before in my whole life. My wife never hinted that she would leave me. Everything that I touched from grammar school on was successful. . . .

"Mine was the skid row of success. The physical skid row in any city is miserable. The skid row of success is just as miserable.

"The second way in which, perhaps, I differ from some other alcoholics is this: many alcoholics state that they didn't particularly like the taste of alcohol, but that they liked the effect. I loved alcohol! I used to like to get it on my fingers so I could lick them and get another taste. I had a lot of fun drinking. I enjoyed it immensely. And then one ill-defined day, one that I can't recall, I stepped across the line that alcoholics know so well, and from that day on drinking was miserable. When a few drinks made me feel good before I went over that line, those same drinks now made me wretched. In an attempt to get over that feeling, there was a quick onslaught of a greater number of drinks, and then all was lost. Alcohol failed to serve the purpose. . . .

"Doctors have been notoriously unsuccessful in helping alcoholics. They have contributed fantastic amounts of time and work to our problem, but they aren't able, it seems, to arrest either your alcoholism or mine.

"And the clergy have tried hard to help us, but we haven't been helped. And the psychiatrist has had thousands of couches, and has put you and me on them many, many times, but he hasn't helped us very much, though he has tried hard; and we owe the clergy and the doctor and the psychiatrist a deep debt of gratitude, but they haven't helped our alcoholism, except in a rare few instances. But—Alcoholics Anonymous has helped.

"What is this power that AA possesses? This curative power? I don't know what it is. I suppose the doctor might say, 'This is psychosomatic medicine.' I suppose the psychiatrist might say, 'This is benevolent interpersonal relations.' I suppose others would say, 'This is group psychotherapy.'

"To me it is God."

Dr. Earle M., 1955, in *Alcoholics Anonymous,*
the Big Book of Alcoholics Anonymous

My special thanks to all the hundreds of AA members who have been part of my recovery through the years.

Thanks, too, to Lucy Barry Robe for being a very helpful editor and good friend, to Jane Thomas Noland for overseeing the entire project in such a gentle and warm way, and to Dave Smith, Jim Milam, Barbara Stern, and Doug Talbot for their encouragement and support.

Author's Introduction

A great deal has been written about the recovering alcoholic's first thirty days of sobriety and even about the rest of that first year. Far less has been published about recovery thereafter, as though, in some miraculous way, recovery should take care of itself. And often, in fact, it does.

However, it seemed to me that a book about long-term sobriety could be useful—the trials, tribulations, disappointments, doubts, fears, and apprehensions, as well as the joys, pleasures, rewards, and increasing inner growth. For this reason, I decided to write my personal odyssey of sobriety over the last thirty-five years, using the "Four I's of Recovery" as my stepping stones.

I first heard of the Four I's of Recovery from the late George H., one of the original hundred members of Alcoholics Anonymous. He came to California in 1950 from the Akron–Cleveland area and settled in Sausalito, on the north side of the Golden Gate Bridge. George, a close friend of AA co-founder Dr. Bob S., explained the Four I's of Recovery to the late Alex McC. and me at his home in 1953.

"The first 'I' is Infatuation," George said. "The second is Irritability, the third, Inventiveness, and the fourth, Insight.

"The *Infatuation* period, sometimes called the 'pink cloud,' is felt deeply by most AA members in their relief over discovering sobriety. Not all people, however, come into AA relieved," he said. "Some are irritable, tense, and nervous. They need time to become infatuated with the Program. But the vast majority of alcoholics in

AA eventually feel infatuated by the whole process—the pink cloud of relief."

George then went on to say that after a few months or years of sobriety, the recovering alcoholic experiences a free-floating feeling of *Irritability,* the second 'I.' "During this period, some AA members become unreasonable, tense, and critical of everybody and everything. They make scathing remarks about meetings, meeting chairmen, and the manner in which meetings are conducted. They are critical of the Big Book and believe it should be rewritten. At times, they even feel alienated from the entire AA fellowship."

In time, the third 'I' enters the picture—the period of *Inventiveness.* In this phase, George said, "the alcoholic devises new ways to try to change AA. In fact, he may start new sorts of groups and meetings, and attempt to reorganize the structure of AA into the way he thinks 'it *should* be.' "

Finally, the fourth 'I' evolves—the period of *Insight,* which dawns when a recovering alcoholic realizes that, although different, we are all in the same boat, brothers and sisters slowly making our way toward an expanding awareness about life and living in a sober state. "This fourth period is one of growing Insight into what AA really is all about, and is a beautiful interval," said George.

George believed that virtually all AA members go through these four phases, which can vary in time from months to years, and which dovetail into one another, creating a continuity.

I had my last drink on June 15, 1953. I have experienced the joys as well as the struggles of a growing, long-term sobriety. The Four I's of Recovery have always intrigued me, and I have personally—and intensely—experienced each phase. Perhaps some readers will identify with my experiences. Some AA members experience the Four I's of Recovery to a very mild degree. Others experience the Four I's with enormous intensity! I am in the latter group. But I would not replace my intensity of living for a world of even-keeled calmness. I like where I have been and where I am today.

I hope that this book will stimulate discussion in AA groups about long-term sobriety. And perhaps it will offer an intriguing feeling of unfolding, as well as comfort and hope, to any wayward AA member who might want to leave our Program after several years of sobriety. I realize that's a big order, but it seems to me that someone ought to give it a try . . . and that's what this book is about.

The Glow and the Guilt

"Bob's drinking started while he was a student at Dartmouth College. He had a large capacity for alcohol during his undergraduate years, and by the time he was in medical school, drinking had become a problem."

About **Bob S., M.D.,** co-founder of AA,
*Pass It On—The Story of Bill Wilson and How
the AA Message Reached the World*

I grew up in San Francisco with parents who were periodic alcoholics. My dad, an electrical engineer, never drank at home; he'd get drunk about once a month. My ma, who ran a rooming house, would get drunk two or three times a year for a couple of days. During dry intervals, they kept no alcohol at home. And when they were drinking, I was too busy feeling apprehensive about them to tackle drinking myself. But how I hungered to try!

My first drink, when I was fifteen, resulted in my first drunk.

That summer of 1926 a friend and I went to Guerneville, a resort on a river sixty miles north of San Francisco, specifically to try booze. We rented a tent with two cots, bought four quarts of wine from a bootlegger (this was during Prohibition), and drank from the bottles. I finished my quart promptly, and I liked it! This is from Heaven, I thought. I looked over at my friend. Although he had drunk only half of his bottle, he frightened me. He seemed in a trance—sitting bolt upright on the edge of his cot, staring straight forward with wide-open, filmy eyes.

"What's the trouble?" I asked him in a loud voice.

That must have jiggled the air sufficiently, for he wobbled momentarily, then plopped over on his bunk. I thought he had died! I became panicky. I was only fifteen; it was illegal to drink booze, and had my parents discovered this escapade, they would have come down on me like a ton of bricks. I didn't know what to do. After a few moments, I approached my friend and cautiously shook him. To my relief, he mumbled. Then I realized that he had simply passed out from being drunk, for I'd seen my parents drunk and knew the signs. Wearily, I lifted his legs up onto the cot and covered him with a blanket.

Never had I felt so lost and lonely. I didn't know what to do next. I was, of course, tipsy from consuming that quart of wine.

For a brief interval I walked outside, stumbling down the path between the rows of tents. The clarity of the bright, starlit sky seemed to reassure me. But back in the tent, sitting on my cot, I shook with depression, loneliness, and fear. All was deadly quiet. Suddenly I spied my friend's unfinished bottle of wine and the other two unopened quarts. Well, I thought, for the first of many times to come, I'll just drink a little more. And I did. I drank the rest of my friend's bottle and also the other two quarts. Initially I was caught up in a glorious, magical glow. But gradually I became unaware of my surroundings, and I must have passed out.

When I woke the next morning, I was still fully dressed, covered with vomit, and experiencing my first terrible hangover. I not only felt awful, but I also carried a deep burden of guilt. I never liked wine much for the rest of my drinking career!

But other kinds of alcohol were to become close friends. Throughout my life, whenever I drank, I drank heavily. My tolerance for alcohol was always high. I drank in high school, college, and medical school, and whenever I drank, I drank to get drunk. I graduated from medical school in 1939, and then completed a five-year postgraduate training in obstetrics and gynecology, plus an additional three-year training program in psychiatry. Fortuitously, however, the drinking intervals in these early days were spaced reasonably far apart.

In the late 1930s, drug companies distributed drugs of all sorts to physicians, to be given out to their patients. Neither drug companies nor doctors were very concerned about addiction in those days. I sampled each drug and liked them all. But one in particular turned me on like a Christmas tree: Benzedrine! I have always been highly energetic, but "bennies," as they were called, seemed to quadruple my accomplishments. I had a ball all jazzed up on bennies, and when I combined them with booze, they were just what I was looking for.

In time, booze and bennies became my constant companions either to "take me up" or to "bring me down" or both, sometimes at the same time. This combination, in varying doses, lasted until my final day of drinking and drug-taking.

Unlike many alcoholics, I didn't drink when I was depressed or when I had a problem. At those times, I was out fighting the world. But when I felt good, I drank and took drugs to go even higher, to feel better and more energetic than I was already. I loved the taste of alcohol and the effect of bennies. I savored the burning sensation of alcohol in my throat and stomach.

If someone said, "Let's have *a* drink," I'd feel sort of ill. I would think, *A drink? What for?*—and usually decline the invitation. One or two drinks made no sense to me. But if I could anticipate an entire evening of drinking, with no limit on time or quantity, I'd be eager and ready to go.

Eventually my episodes of heavy drinking and drug-taking increased and became closer together. I experienced shakes and sweats, repeated blackouts, and morning drinking (on weekends only). But strange as it may seem today, I had no inkling that I was alcoholic. At that time all alcoholics were considered skid row habitues. I was hardly on skid row. Yes, I knew that I was in trouble with alcohol, but I failed to connect the shakes, sweats, and blackouts with my drinking. I decided, instead, that I was suffering from "hyperventilation," and took large doses of phenobarbital and ammonium chloride (at that time the appropriate medical treatment for hyperventilation) to treat my shakes and sweats. A physician can easily misdiagnose his own case!

I was aware that I had difficulty stopping drinking and staying stopped. I went "on the wagon" many, many times. But during my last years of drinking, I never stayed on the wagon for more than seven days. One Sunday evening, I recall telling myself that I was going to stop drinking for good. Five days later, on Friday, I came home, filled a glass with vodka, and, as I drank it down, said to myself, I thought you said you were going to stop drinking! I simply could not stay on the wagon and I didn't know why, but the diagnosis of alcoholism never occurred to me.

Even in the last stages of my alcoholism, I had enough self-discipline to avoid drinking in my office or at the hospital during office hours. Never did I shirk my professional responsibilities. I had a beautiful office, and in the lower right drawer of my desk, I kept a bottle of vodka, a bottle of Scotch, and a bottle of bourbon. In the lower left drawer were six glasses that my nurses had given me as a gift. The last two hours in the office were miserable, but never did I take that first drink until *after* my last patient had left. Then I'd go into my consultation room, close the door, fill a glass with vodka, and drink. What a relief!

I stopped at bars en route home, but I made it a point never to stay very long in any one bar. One drink, at most two, then on to the next bar. I was a physician, and I didn't want to be seen or recognized. In spite of this circuitous route of bar drinking, I never deduced that I was alcoholic. And yet I *was* apprehensive. I sensed that something very strange was happening to me.

In general, I was a lone drinker. When I drank in run-down, crummy bars, I'd hide in a corner. I frequented after-hours joints, usually when I was blacked out or partially so. Sometimes I spent the night in such places, and would wake up the next morning surrounded by an array of strangers. I couldn't remember where I was or how I got there, and I'd dress quietly and ease out a side door.

At home, too, I was a lone drinker. I usually refused to eat dinner with the family, preferring to drink alone in the sitting room. When I drank, my appetite vanished. Late in the evening, I would drag myself outdoors to our barbecue area. With a fire blazing, I would lie on a lounge with my bottle. Sometimes I lay there all night—drinking, drugging, scheming, dreaming—bathed in globs of self-pity, which was coupled with an inner excitement probably induced by Benzedrine.

Oddly, if I stayed at the hospital, I felt safe from the urge to drink. The hospital was a sort of soothing mother for me. I stayed there many times, even if I had no medical reason to do so, in order to escape the urge to drink. There I felt safe from myself, and without booze or drugs, I could relax and dream my dreams. I have never understood why the hospital was such a haven, but my heart seemed to be at rest there.

As the years passed, I became bewildered and filled with remorse. My world was topsy-turvy much of the time, yet I could easily crawl back into my professional role and perform well. My innate energy was high, and my capacity to fulfill my professional duties and most of my home duties kept me from recognizing that I was dependent on alcohol and bennies. I believed that I was a normal drinker, like "everyone else." And sometimes I was, until an all-night joint or the barbecue area beckoned me. But I never drank until I had signed out to my physician-partner and knew that my patients would be in safe hands.

I had a great obstetrics and gynecology partner, who frequently covered for me. For example, he would carry my patient load if I returned from a medical convention two or three days late.

But sometimes he couldn't cover. In the late 1940s I was invited to Harvard to address its obstetrical and gynecological faculty on the new birthing method. I flew the Red Eye Special from San Francisco and arrived in Boston around 10:00 A.M. I shaved and showered at my hotel, but I had very little to do until evening. So at about one o'clock, I went to a bar and ordered a drink, and by five o'clock I was fairly drunk.

Suddenly I remembered my Harvard lecture that evening. I was panic-stricken. Incredibly, I had forgotten! (This is a prime example of how the alcoholic will get drunk at the most inappropriate times and getting drunk before a presentation to Harvard faculty is, indeed, a most inappropriate time!)

I went to a restaurant, ate, and drank several cups of coffee. Since I still had a couple of hours before my lecture, I took a brisk walk. I began to sober up but not enough. I recall my presentation that night with anguish. My tongue was thick, my thinking unclear, and it was apparent to me and to the audience that I was a little drunk. I was never invited back to Harvard. Years later, I made amends to Professor Duncan Reed and others on the faculty. To a degree, I hope, I have been forgiven.

My partner and I were good friends. He protected me, perhaps too much, from the results of my drinking. But eventually he could no longer stand my antics and sadly, in late 1952, we dissolved the partnership. Then I was *really* alone. I hesitate to contemplate how close I came to alcohol and drug disaster. How long my luck would have continued, I don't know. Six months after my partner and I separated, I felt a horror expanding within me, although I still did not identify it as alcohol-induced.

'This Is Your Last Drink!'

" . . . Dr. Bob had worked out a grim routine that permitted him to drink and somehow still maintain his medical practice. Careful never to go near the hospital while he was drinking, he would stay sober until four o'clock in the afternoon. 'It was really a horrible nightmare, this earning money, getting liquor, smuggling it home, getting drunk, morning jitters, taking large doses of sedatives to make it possible for me to earn more money, and so on ad nauseam,' he wrote. 'I used to promise my wife, my friends, and my children that I would drink no more—promises which seldom kept me sober through the day, though I was very sincere when I made them.' "

About **Bob S., M.D.**, co-founder of AA,
*Pass It On—The Story of Bill Wilson and How
the AA Message Reached the World*

My last day of drinking and using drugs was June 15, 1953. It started at Sam's Restaurant and Bar, about twenty miles from my home. Sam's was a high-class hangout. I drank there many times. I loved to drink on weekend mornings. That day I ordered a Waring blender of vodka fizzes and three double vodka martinis. I haven't the foggiest notion why I ordered that many martinis, why they were doubles, or why I also ordered a blender full of fizzes. It just seemed like a reasonable idea.

That day I did not black out. I "browned" out: I remember a few events. I can't recall driving home to Mill Valley, but I do remember being there at about noon. It was a sunny day, and I relaxed on my deck with giant-sized Alexanders. About two o'clock, for reasons unknown to me, I visited Harry, a college fraternity brother who lived nearby. I knew that he had been in serious trouble with alcohol. However, I did not see him for help with *my* drinking. Nor did I go looking for Alcoholics Anonymous. As I recall, he said to me, "You know, I've been in trouble with alcohol, but I've stopped drinking."

"Is that so," I said.

"Yes, and I've joined AA. Do you know about Alcoholics Anonymous?"

In 1941 I had read an article about AA written by Jack Alexander. (The article was published in the *Saturday Evening Post* March 1, 1941. AA's membership quadrupled by 1942.) I'd been struck by the fact that one founder of AA was a physician, like me, and I had identified with Dr. Bob. I told Harry I'd read the Alexander article, but that was all I knew about AA.

Harry said, "I've been sober in AA for seven months, and it's a great relief. You know, my wife left me. And I've been in jail just too many times." He beamed. "But now I feel good." Actually, I had known all this. I congratulated him, thinking that I might investigate AA from a medical standpoint. He gave me several pieces of AA literature to read at home.

I don't remember driving home, but I do recall sitting on my deck around four o'clock. I was so drunk that I simply could not decipher the words, so I asked my wife to read the AA pamphlets to me.

One was a series of questions and bits of advice directed to the drinker who was considering sobriety. Two statements jolted me: "Don't stop drinking for anybody else except *yourself*," and "Don't consider *yourself* a martyr because *you* stopped drinking." I felt as if somebody had slapped me across the face with a wet beer towel. I broke down and cried.

Crying in those days was a frequent occurrence for me. (I had no idea then that this emotional instability results from alcoholic drinking.) For example, if I heard Bing Crosby sing on my car radio, I would cry. If I saw a cloud in the sky, I'd cry. If I looked at the sky and did NOT see a cloud, I'd cry. I'd cry at the sight of my wife and daughter. (Doubtless—they looked at me and cried too!) In any event, that's where I was—emotional, bewildered, and weeping.

After several minutes, my wife patted me on the back and said, "I'm sure you'll be all right." My sobs subsided slowly. With a final pat, she withdrew to the house. I sat alone for another ten minutes, deeply depressed and lost.

It was about six o'clock, time to build the charcoal barbecue fire. With great effort, I sloppily climbed the fifteen outside steps to the barbecue area. One finger of my drink remained in my glass. "This will never do," I murmured. "This little bit of drink won't keep me going. I'd better go down to the kitchen and make another, to have while I'm building the fire."

At that moment, I had what AA calls a "spiritual awakening." It's almost impossible to describe, but as I turned on that top stair, an explosion seemed to occur inside me. A tremendous surge of pain flashed through my body. I was in agony. I cannot account medically for the cause of this pain or of the explosive feeling.

I paused in wonder, and then I heard these words: "This is your last drink!"

Now, that statement wasn't quite accurate, because I didn't even finish the drink in my hand. *I had already had my last drink!*

"What's happening to me?" I muttered aloud. At that instant, I became absolutely clear and sober, as sober as I am today. One second before, I had been so drunk I could hardly stand up. Now I was not. How I transferred that quickly from a drunken state to a sober one, I'm sure I don't know. But *in that moment of clarity, I realized that alcohol and drugs had created all of my problems.* I thought, for the very first time, *You are a drunk; you are an alcoholic!*

A bantam breeze blew across my forehead. I felt light as a feather, as if a heavy overcoat had slipped from my shoulders. The sun was brighter; the world seemed new. I felt free, *absolutely* free.

In my temporary clarity, as I came to know that I was alcoholic, the craving to take another drink disappeared from me totally, never to return.

I realized that something very big and very strange had happened to me. Something far beyond my control, my reach, my understanding. Without asking for it, physical sobriety had been handed to me on a golden platter. I had been transported to a new plane of existence. I was a new person.

An instant later, I slipped back into drunkenness.

I woke up early the next afternoon. To my surprise, I had no craving to drink. That feeling was entirely new. What a wonder, I thought. But knowing now that I was alcoholic, I also knew that I needed help. I decided to see my fraternity brother Harry again.

"I realized that I was in trouble with alcohol after I saw you yesterday afternoon," I told Harry. "I think I should go to that AA of yours. Will you take me?"

"By all means," he replied.

"Were you trying to convince me yesterday that I'm alcoholic?"

"No," he said. "In spite of the fact that you were rather drunk, I didn't know that you were in trouble with alcohol."

Harry took me to my first AA meeting the following week. This meeting was a landmark, the start of a deep and never-ending infatuation with Alcoholics Anonymous and all the people in it.

Physical sobriety was given to me on June 15, 1953. However, acquiring emotional sobriety has been another story! I was destined to experience great joys and wonderment, as well as periods of excruciating emotional pain, in the ensuing years, as my heart and soul became deeply enmeshed with the AA way of life.

INFATUATION WITH AA

The Infatuation Period

". . . Somewhat to our surprise, staying sober turns out not to be the grim, wet-blanket experience we had expected! While we were drinking, a life without alcohol seemed like no life at all. But for most members of AA, living sober is really living a joyous experience. We much prefer it to the troubles we had with drinking."

Living Sober

In early sobriety, infatuation with AA and its members can represent a sort of romance. Most members that I have known feel this way early in AA.

As we awaken from a drunken/drugged sleep into sobriety, a sense of love and devotion for AA develops. At times this can be rather extreme and occasionally even unreal. AA and all its members seem truly beautiful and glorious.

For many recovering alcoholics, hyperactivity replaces the old sense of lethargy. Intervals of doubt, depression, and fatigue may temporarily crop up to mar the shiny surfaces of new-found sobriety.

The Infatuation period can be strenuous, while also rewarding and lovely. A feeling of being "well-groomed inside" develops, but because we are on shaky legs, our happiness is fragile and can shatter easily. The "bottom," in which the ego is temporarily demolished to allow us to surrender to our alcoholism, really represents the "top." If only we could stay up there, life would be beautiful. But the persistent ego repeatedly rears its ugly head; we must recognize, accept, and deal with it. The ups and downs of recovery during the Infatuation period are well known to all AA members.

I have always loved AA. Even though I have been critical of the Program at times, my devotion has always been constant and enormous. My own infatuation with AA has basically never left me, as the following pages will attest.

HYPERACTIVITY AND
HALF MEASURES IN AA

"Sometimes a newcomer's first A.A. meeting may be that of a group which has no one with whom he or she can identify . . ."

Milton A. Maxwell, Ph.D., The A.A. Experience

AA meetings were rather small in the early 1950s. There were only five people at my first—all men. The Tuesday Night Mill Valley AA Group met in Wesley Hall at the Methodist Church. In the center of the room was a standard four-by-eight banquet table, bare except for a copy of the "Big Book," *Alcoholics Anonymous.* At the left end of the table sat Clark B., our community butcher, who was a gentle, easy-going, lovable man. At the right end sat Shorty R., a five-foot-tall carpenter, bald, irritable, but likeable, and a devoted AA member. Across from me was Vern W., the local baker, who was an old-timer in AA, and beside me sat my friend Harry H., a self-styled mechanic/inventor, who had a small independent income.

I glanced around the table and realized that I, the Great Physician, was in the company of a butcher, a carpenter, a baker, and a kind of ne'er-do-well mechanic! I considered them to be four "inferiors."

I excused myself for a few moments, walked out to the church-yard, stood under a lovely linden tree, and asked myself, Do you mean to tell me that I—a physician, a professor at the medical school, a fellow of the American College of Surgeons and of the International College of Surgeons, a diplomate of the American

Board of Obstetrics and Gynecology, board-qualified in psychiatry, vice-president of the American Association of Marital and Family Therapists—must attend that meeting, in order to let a butcher, a baker, a carpenter, and a mechanic, help make a man out of me?

And a little voice inside replied, "Yes, you certainly do. Get back in there."

I returned to the meeting. And despite my resentment, omnipotent posture, and egocentric attitude, the four men made me feel wanted and included. When I went home that evening, I felt elated and invigorated. Never has a physician been so grateful to a butcher, a carpenter, a baker, and a mechanic. Unhappily, my former fraternity brother Harry got drunk many months later, and died from alcoholism. But the other three men continued to be enormously helpful to my recovery. Harry got me there—the others did the rest.

In those days, most people came into AA after suffering enormous losses—wives, children, money, jobs, etc. Not me. I had plenty of clinical symptoms of alcoholism, such as shakes, sweats, frequent blackouts, increased heavy drinking and drug taking, but I had never been arrested, jailed, or treated for alcoholism in a hospital. For years, success had been at my side. I'd always been elected president of my various student bodies, beginning in grammar school and continuing through high school, college, my fraternity, medical school. I had been voted the man most likely to succeed in both college and medical school. I'd been admitted to medical organizations at a young age, before most of my colleagues.

Despite my alcoholism, I had become increasingly successful, and earned more and more money. In fact, the last year of my drinking I made more money that I'd ever made before. But success was becoming a serious problem for me. I'd begun to believe my own publicity, that I was a "special" person—a sort of God. I had begun to think that all good things must, therefore, come from *me*!

As do all alcoholics, I came to AA with great inner turmoil and trouble. I had had enough to drink. I had had enough prestige and success. I had had everything—yet I had nothing. Inside, I felt empty, dry, shriveled. I was isolated, lonely, and desolate. I hated my success, my prestige, my money—but mostly I hated myself. I desperately wanted peace.

I had been elated when I first realized I was alcoholic, because alcoholism satisfactorily explained all this inner turmoil. Yet, after attending my first AA meeting, I worried that I might not have had enough "external" troubles, or lost enough materially, to qualify for membership. I desperately wanted and needed AA, so I decided to talk to an expert: Jack I., secretary of the San Francisco Central AA Fellowship, who later became my close friend.

"I very much want to join AA," I told Jack. "I've had great inner turmoil and about all the trouble with alcohol that I can stand. But I haven't lost everything. I wonder if you folks in AA will accept me anyway?"

Jack was a benevolent and direct man. "Of course we will, Earle. You're as welcome as the flowers in May."

That did it for me! What a relief to know that I could consider myself a "bona fide" AA member, even though my external and physical problems had been less dramatic than those of AA members I'd met.

My *inner* troubles, however, were identical to others' in the fellowship. As I see it, all emotional and spiritual "bottoms" in AA are the same. Despair is despair is despair. To me, my despair was deep and formidable.

For five years in the late 1930s and early 1940s, I had been in psychoanalysis, trying to help myself emotionally. And I *did* receive some help, but the root cause of my trouble—my alcoholism—was *never* addressed during my psychoanalysis. Consequently, it progressed unabated.

When I first joined AA, there were only a handful of meetings in our area, and I attended them all. (In time, of course, other meetings were established, and I went to them as well.) I considered the Tuesday Night Mill Valley AA meeting my "home" group. Every Sunday evening, my elation would begin to build. I anticipated the Tuesday meeting like a child waiting for Santa Claus.

Discovering that I was alcoholic was a golden find. I was relieved to have found AA, and I plunged into the Program with great zest and joy. I had always been an exceedingly active person, but the discovery of AA gave me an energy boost which surpassed any high I'd had from alcohol, Benzedrine, and a sprinkling of other drugs. My early AA "hyperactivity" was a pleasure and I loved it!

I volunteered for the group's "scut" work. I bought the cookies and doughnuts, took them to the meeting, arranged the chairs and coffee cups, checked that we had sufficient literature, and, in general, was a willing servant to the group. After each meeting, I put the chairs and table back in their places, washed the cups and saucers, and left Wesley Hall in good repair. Without thinking twice about it, I performed these chores for about two-and-a-half years. Finally one day Clark suggested that I allow a newer member to take over, since this kind of work enhanced sobriety for newcomers. Eventually I did turn my duties over to a new member, but with some reluctance, for I tenaciously clung to the image of myself as a perennial newcomer.

After I had been in AA for about a month, I was invited to some meetings which were not the traditional AA meetings I knew, but were attended by some other AA members. One group was called "Jesus as Teacher," from the book by the same name by Sharman, and was devoted to studying and understanding the *teachings* of Jesus, not His supposed divinity. Many members were one-upmanship players. I was in early sobriety—still toxic, confused, and bewildered. I thought the Jesus as Teacher group was normal activity for AA members, so I joined it.

About four months later, though I acted elated, I carried a dull heaviness inside. From time to time, I seemed to be floating up into the sky, actually studying the heavens and the clouds. This was not the typical AA "pink cloud." It was another kind of cloud—one higher than God. My misery increased.

I approached Clark, a sort of father figure in my Mill Valley AA Group. These days I would consider him one of my sponsors, along with Bill W., Jack I., and Shorty R., but we didn't talk much about sponsors in California back then. "Clark, there's something terribly wrong with me," I said. "I've been in AA for four months, but I might just as well be drunk as feel the way I do right now. I'm *miserable!*"

Clark said, "Earle, let me get you a cup of coffee." With coffee in hand, he led me to a couple of chairs in the far corner of Wesley Hall. "Earle, you know I'm very proud of you, and what you've done," he said. "You're the only doctor we have around here. We don't get many professional people in our groups. But you know, we have an organization here in Mill Valley known as Alcoholics Anonymous. Why don't you join it?"

I gazed at him in shocked disbelief. "But Clark, I *do* belong to AA. I mean, what do you think I've been doing the last four months?" He smiled. "That's difficult to say, but I'll do my best. The other group you're in is okay. There's nothing wrong in going to those meetings, if you want, for philosophical information. But it might be wise for you to do some more studying in *Alcoholics Anonymous*. You're in an early stage of your sobriety, so AA is *more* important." Then he quietly asked, "Have you ever read the Big Book?"

"Indeed I have. Three times," I replied proudly.

"You don't learn very readily, do you?" he chuckled.

We both laughed. I began to see that my years of academic training apparently weren't much use in this situation. I said, "Maybe I don't, but what especially do you mean? I don't understand. What would you do if you were in my shoes?"

"I'd go home, open the Big Book to page 70, and re-read it," he said with a gentle smile.

In those days, we referred to Chapter Five as "Page 70" rather than by the title "How It Works." (In later editions of the Big Book, page 70 became page 58.) Since we read page 70 at the beginning of each AA meeting, I knew exactly what he meant. I thanked Clark, and went home to follow his suggestion with gusto.

I opened my Big Book to page 70 and read as follows:

"Rarely have we seen a person fail who has thoroughly followed our path. . . ."

I paused. The book said *thoroughly* followed our path!

". . . Those who do not recover are people who cannot or will not completely give themselves. . ."

Completely give themselves!

". . . to this simple program, usually men and women who are constitutionally incapable of being honest with themselves. There are such unfortunates. They are not at fault; they seem to have been born that way. They are naturally incapable of grasping and developing a manner of living which demands rigorous honesty. . . ."

Rigorous honesty!

Finally it sank into my thick skull. Yes, I'd heard the words many times before, but never *felt* them with such intensity. Other sentences jumped out at me:

". . . If you have decided you want what we have and are willing to go to any length to get it then you are ready to take certain steps."

"At some of these we balked . . . With all the earnestness at our command, we beg of you to be fearless and thorough from the very start. . . ."

"Some of us have tried to hold on to our old ideas and the result was nil until we let go absolutely. . . ."

"Remember that we deal with alcohol—cunning, baffling, powerful!. . . ."

"Half measures availed us nothing. . . ."

The Big Book did not say half measures availed us *half*. The book was very clear: half measures availed us *nothing*.

"*. . . We stood at the turning point. We asked His protection and care with complete abandon . . . .*"

"*Here are the steps we took, which are suggested as a Program of Recovery:*"

I redigested the Twelve Steps (page 234). I learned to review parts of the Big Book every day. I discovered that it did not tell me to *do* anything. There were *no* requirements in AA. AA didn't even tell me that I had to stop drinking, or that I had to be sober. It only *suggested* a program to use as a guide if I wanted sobriety and a daily spiritual life.

GOD, AS WE UNDERSTAND HIM

" 'I want to make something easy for you,' he {Dr. Bob} said. 'Try to find
your own God as you understand him.' 'I remember one story he repeated
over and over,' said Ed {an AA old-timer}. 'It was about this boy who
burned his hand. The doctor dressed it and bandaged it. When he took
the bandage off, the boy's hand was healed. The little boy said, "You're
wonderful, Doctor. You cure everybody, don't you?" "No, I don't," the
doctor replied. "I just dress the wound. God heals it." ' "

Dr. Bob and the Good Old Timers

Spiritual thoughts were new to me. I was knowledgeable about
psychoanalysis and other forms of philosophical thought, from such
thinkers as Jung, Freud, Horney, Sullivan, Sartre, Camus, Jaspers,
and Heidegger. But I had never given serious consideration to
matters of a spiritual nature. Actually I thought they were rather
silly. However, after my overwhelming spiritual experience on the
last day of my drinking, I became more receptive to spiritual ideas.

I believe that almost all AA members struggle with our Third
Step: "Made a decision to turn our will and our lives over to the
care of God as we understood Him."

I met Jimmy B. in 1957. He was one of the first hundred AA
members, whose own struggle effected a change in the Third Step's
phrasing. Jimmy B. was a pillar of the Program. In San Diego he
very colorfully described to me how, in the early days of AA, he
refused to bow before a God of the Oxford Movement.

The Oxford Movement was a religious organization, most
popular in the nineteenth century but still active in the 1930s,

which focused on many "sins," including drinking alcohol. Abstinence from alcohol was only part of that program. Bill W. and some other future AA members joined the Oxford Movement in unsuccessful attempts to stay sober. The Oxford Movement's Six Steps were used in the development of AA's Twelve Steps.

Jimmy had his own ideas about God. They were different. His resistance caused the phrase "as we understood Him" to be added to the Third Step. Bill W. later said that this had been done in concert with other AA members. The point has never been conclusively settled, but in my opinion, Jimmy should have credit for the added phrase.

My own first inkling of God, as we understand Him, came to me in my office. I had operated on a woman, removing a large benign uterine tumor. Six days later I took the sutures from her wound, and the day after that I discharged her from the hospital. That afternoon the patient's husband phoned. In expressing his gratitude for the care I had given his wife, he stated, "Thank you very much, doctor, for curing my wife."

Those words, *"Thank you for curing my wife"* affected me in a new way. I had been thanked many times before by patients and their families, but this time the words had new meaning.

I asked myself, Did *I cure* her? I knew the value of my diagnostic ability and surgical talent. But could I really tell myself that *I* had *cured* her? When I removed her sutures, the wound was tightly healed; yet had I removed them within the first forty-eight hours after surgery, the wound would have fallen apart. Yes, I knew the microscopic anatomy of healing, and the principles of surgery to facilitate healing, but had *I* really cured her? Each morning after her operation, I had made hospital rounds with the residents and nurses. A brief examination would reassure both me and the patient. Then I would dress the wound, write a few orders in her chart, and go on my way. The nurses had spent more time with my patient than I did. If anyone had cured her, *they* had. And yet, even with my surgical skills and their tender, loving care, I could not really account for *why* that wound had healed and *why* she was now well.

I pondered these questions for a week or two. Finally I decided that everyone has an individual tendency to get well, to heal. Whatever it was, this healing factor had turned the trick.

I asked myself, With the help of this patient and her husband, have I discovered "a Power greater than myself"? I became excited and enthralled by my find. I could see that, among many other things, *God must be that healing power in each of us.*

Ever since then, I've watched scores of patients recover, and marveled at how the Healing Power inside them not only directs this healing, but also works in concert with my medical and surgical skills. I am merely a part of it all.

Not long after that, I deduced that if this Healing Power could effect a physical cure, why not also an emotional one? Physical and emotional healing are both at work in recovery from alcoholism. I decided that this must be the "spiritual fitness" to which the Big Book refers. That grateful phone call in my office years ago remains clear as a beacon light and represents, for me, God as I understand Him. Spiritual fitness became an observable feature in my patients, one which I could watch daily with wonder, and a vital, living truth which helped me solidify my sobriety.

I could relate many more examples of how, over the years, I extended my original insight about God as I understand Him. But one, in particular, stands out. I was driving home in very heavy traffic one day when a car suddenly pulled in front of me and almost hit me. I was forced to swerve into the next lane. Luckily space was available. If not, we would have had a very serious accident—both of us were traveling at about fifty miles per hour.

While recovering from that close call, a thought occurred to me: If I had been forced to crash into another automobile, and if my hands had been seriously injured as a result, my surgical skills would have been destroyed. My operating days would have ended. At that moment, I could see that my surgical abilities were only "loaned" to me. I do not own them; they can be withdrawn. My professional skills are not mine to flaunt, but to use and nurture. The only interest that I must pay on that "loan" is wise surgical judgment—not a bad business arrangement!

I didn't know this in the 1950s, but in the later years of my sobriety, and with reasonably mature thinking, I realized that the *very act* of "turning over" one's "will and life" is really a form of hanging on. I learned, with force, that I cannot "take" AA's third Step; it has to "dawn" on me—to evolve of its own volition.

Two months before I joined Alcoholics Anonymous, I had decided to stop practicing obstetrics, so that I would not have to be on call at all hours and could drink uninterrupted. I'd planned to devote myself solely to surgical gynecology. After joining AA, I decided to continue with these professional plans. Even sober, I liked doing regularly scheduled surgery, free from the constraints of being on obstetrical call.

However, I was still obligated to my obstetrical patients for the next six or seven months. I cared for them willingly. While waiting for a patient to deliver her baby, I'd spend the long hours reading *Alcoholics Anonymous*. I memorized the Fifth Chapter and other smaller segments of the book, as well as the Prayer of St. Francis (popular in AA) and AA's Serenity Prayer.

Every morning I rose at four o'clock, exercised at home for an hour, then drove across the Golden Gate Bridge to swim a quarter of a mile at the Olympic Club in San Francisco. In the club's steam room, I'd repeat Big Book passages to myself, savoring each word. Then I would shower, dress, and drive to the hospital, either to operate and/or to make rounds on patients recovering from surgery.

Scrubbing for surgery, I would murmur to myself, "Guide these hands." After the patient had been anesthetized, I would ask each member of the surgical team, in turn, "Are you ready?" Operating personnel knew that my only intent was to draw their attention to the operating area. Silence was broken only for a justified reason. If things proved difficult during surgery, or if there was a question about which way I should proceed, I would pack the wound with warm lap tapes (pieces of gauze material that had been soaked in warm saline solution), move a step or two away from the operating table, close my eyes, and ask for guidance. After a brief interval, the answer inevitably came to me. At the end of the operation, as we lifted the patient to the gurney, I would murmur to the heavens, "Thanks."

I'd go to the recovery room with the patient and gently take her pulse, hoping that her Healing Power and mine might connect, and thereby hasten her recovery. Perhaps this routine seems ridiculous, unreasonable, or childish to some people, but it always helped me and seemed to help my patients. The meditations of the morning and throughout the day were invaluable to me.

In my early sobriety, I underwent a kind of transformation: religion grabbed me. This was part of my Infatuation phase. In those days, I didn't know the difference between religion (didactic rules) and spiritual principles (founded on inspiration). Nonetheless, for a long period in my life, religions of all sorts interested me.

My parents gave me a duly inscribed Bible when I first joined AA. My father was essentially an agnostic. My mother was a Methodist, though her religious leanings were erratic. My mother was overjoyed to see the change in me. Her joy, in turn, stimulated me even more, and I bought several Bibles and copies of AA books. I kept copies of the Big Book, *Twelve Steps and Twelve Traditions,* and the King James *New Testament* in my automobile, my obstetrical locker, my surgical locker, my bedside nightstand, and the drawer of my office desk which had previously harbored my alcohol supply!

I read the *New Testament* from beginning to end three times, and became enamored of several sections. Matthew 24, to me, was the intense agony that precedes the instant of emotional change. And Matthew 25 seemed a parable about Twelfth Step work: being rewarded for helping the underling (sheep, goats, and the Kingdom of Heaven).

My early interpretation of these two sections probably would have caused the hair on the head of any theologian to stand straight up on end, but I liked dovetailing these biblical stories into my program for sobriety.

AA member Jim W. gave me Emmett Fox's *The Sermon on the Mount*. This valuable book helped me put to rest many old Biblical terms which had haunted me—terms such as "sin," "evil," and "the wrath of God." Fox explained them in a way which not only appealed to me, but also made me more comfortable with them.

And though I was a rather wayward Protestant, I found great comfort in visiting churches of all kinds, including Jewish synagogues, Catholic cathedrals, and any Protestant church. I now loved long periods of silence and frequently would sit in a church pew alone, drinking in the silence. This, to me, was a form of prayer.

Occasionally I used traditional prayer, but I was not especially comfortable with it. I wasn't *against* it; traditional prayer simply wasn't my way. In the years to come, I would experience many doubts about the traditional religious process. My discomfort with traditional prayer at this early time in AA was a precursor to a long interval of religious doubt. After many years of sobriety, this doubt would filter down to *my own* views of God, spirituality, and how they fit into my own life.

We Live in Solitude, but also Magically Together

Paradoxically, in spite of a high degree of personal confidence on one level, on another I had always felt that I was less than a first-class person, destined to be at the beck and call of others as well as of my own inner demands.

Early one morning in my sixth month of sobriety, alone at our barbecue area, I became painfully aware that I had never really felt "at home" no matter where I lived. I began to cry softly. I felt like a lost child who longed to find his place or home in the world. At the same time I understood that I was a mature adult, who knew to a great degree where he was headed. But that morning, the "lost child" dominated. I sat down and let the pain wash over me. After several minutes, I felt sudden inner peace, as I accepted the fact that I was a child floating in the universe, that I would always be in solitude. And with that acceptance, my pain subsided and disappeared.

The thought popped into my head that the only *real* home I would *ever* have was inside me. External homes such as my house were nice, but they were secondary. At this point, I realized that I had *always* lived in solitude; I just had not been aware of it. By solitude, I don't mean being alone. I don't mean being lonely. I mean simply living in solitude. I liked it! My longing to find "a home" disappeared—after all, I was already home! I was free, and I felt "together."

I further realized that although I can share my feelings with others, I am not a follower. I am my own man. My own person. My feelings of dependence on parents, wives, children, medical practice, religions, AA, and the like evaporated. I became intrigued with making my own way and my own discoveries, within the AA Program and outside of it. The recognition that I live in solitude and am free to be my own person became an integral part of me. It gave me a confidence that has never left me.

My awareness that I live in solitude was one of the more exciting events of my AA Infatuation period. As I saw it, we all live in solitude, for the simple reason that no one else can ever climb inside of us to discover how we *really* feel. However, we are also magically together with others. Like a garden in which each flower is separate and distinct, the flowers together create a unified, land-scaped beauty. Solitude and togetherness join hands.

This may sound paradoxical, but the whole process of recovery in AA is paradoxical:

▲We become powerless in order to gain power.

▲We give up our lives in order to gain a new life.

▲We make amends and thereby feel strong.

▲We rely on a Higher Power in order to live our lives with zest.

It is all a paradox, just as being in solitude together is a paradox.

My Friend Bill W.
and New York AA

". . . Dr. Earle M., . . . {Bill's} close friend, said: 'I felt that he {Bill W.} had no one he could talk with about his far-out spiritual ideas. When I listened to him, he would turn on and become vibrant, and his eyes would shine . . . .' "

Pass It On, The Story of Bill Wilson
and How the A.A. Message Reached the World

In 1953, the first year of my sobriety, I was interested in learning the history of AA (less than two decades old at that time) and about its inner workings. On a business trip to New York, I tentatively approached the AA office at 141 East 44th Street and modestly made my interests known.

The AA office was rather stark, with battleship-gray walls. The receptionist sat behind a counter. There was a telephone switchboard, doubtless the plug-in type common at the time.

I was greeted with open arms by Nell Wing, Bill W.'s beautiful secretary, with whom I still keep in touch today.

Nell introduced me to Eve M., another staffer, who also became a good, lifelong friend. Now sober some forty-plus years, Eve still gives inspiring AA speeches. I heard one in the fall of 1987 in California, and we had a wonderful reunion. This elegant Vassar graduate is more beautiful than ever!

Nell also introduced me to Bill W.

My first impression of Bill was his height: he was six foot three or four. He looked tall and lean, and he dressed neatly in conservative business suits. If you saw him walking down the street, you'd probably think he worked in a stock-and-bond office. He had nice-looking clothes, but they'd get rumpled because he'd get in all kinds of funny positions. He'd put his feet up on his desk, he'd twist around, he'd bend over, he'd slump. I'm sure he had to get his suits pressed every day.

I was awestruck by Bill. He and I shared alcoholic stories, and discovered that we both had found sobriety in a spiritual awakening which could only be described as a "hot flash."

After that Bill and I became very close. We talked frequently, both on the phone and in person.

He was one of my sponsors.

There was hardly a topic that we did not discuss in detail, including alcoholism, drug abuse, sobriety, growth in AA, emotional change, how to use the AA Program in everyday living, and especially how to apply the AA principles in the field of medicine. I took a Fifth Step with Bill. We talked about the marital problems that alcoholics seem to have when they come into the Program (our own marriages were no exception). Bill remained one of my closest and dearest friends until his death in January 1971.

When I met him, Bill was on a high-carbohydrate diet. When visitors came to the office, he liked to take them to a little cafe down the street and buy them cake and ice cream. It was just a one-shot for the visitors, but Bill did it repeatedly. So, of course, he was not in the best of shape.

One day, when I'd known him a year or so, I said, "Bill, let me be a doctor for a minute." I took a nutritional history and when I found out what he was doing, I said, "You know, you're on a protein-deficient diet." I explained that I believed at least 95 percent of all alcoholics were hypoglycemic and should avoid sugar like the plague.

Bill stopped the sugar. He'd order something like a glass of milk at that cafe, while his visitors had ice cream. After that, Bill often said, "I feel better now that my gynecologist has put me on a high-protein diet!"

It would be impossible to relate how much I learned from Bill. He was a spiritual genius, but his feet were planted firmly on the ground. I often communicated by mail with him, Nell, Lib, Eve, Ann, Beth, and others in the New York office. At that time, all in the office except Nell were recovering alcoholics. I wish now that I had saved their letters, but alas, I did not.

I visited New York at the slightest opportunity. I looked specifically for medical meetings to attend in New York, for this meant that I could see my AA friends. They made my early years of sobriety beautiful. Seeing them always gave me an enormous charge, for they were a comforting, mothering group. I'd relate my AA experiences to them with zest and intensity. How my own sobriety was strengthened by them!

Not long after that, I met Marty Mann, recovered alcoholic and founder of the National Council on Alcoholism, who became another lifelong friend. In her 1950 book, *Marty Mann's Primer on Alcoholism,* Marty wrote: *"An alcoholic is someone whose drinking causes a continuing problem in any department in his life."*(p.66). This statement appealed to me, since alcohol had caused continuing problems in many facets of my life.

When I told Marty the impact that her book, and this statement in particular, had made on me, she replied: "That's the longest Twelfth Step call I've ever made!" Although Marty lived on the East Coast and I on the West, we met frequently. She died in 1982, having devoted most of her time and energy during more than forty years of sobriety to helping other alcoholics—including this one!

My boss Bill W. and my friend Earle M.

▲ ▲ ▲ ▲ ▲ ▲ ▲ ▲ ▲

"I think Earle first visited GSO in 1953. At that time it was still called the Alcoholic Foundation; the name was changed to the General Service Board of AA in the fall of 1954.

"Our office was on the second floor of 141 East 44th Street in New York City. We had three large main rooms, the middle one being a reception area that separated the staff from business and clerical activities. At that time, I'd guess that we employed about twenty people, six or seven of whom were AA staff members. The *AA Grapevine* staff was on the first floor of our building.

"Bill W. came to the office pretty regularly, about two days a week. He commuted by train from Bedford Hills. After an office was started for Al-Anon, his wife Lois also spent a day or two a week in New York.

"I handled Bill's work and other secretarial duties, and I was also office receptionist, so my desk was in the reception area. There,

for eight years, I enjoyed greeting and talking to visitors from all over the world.

"I clearly remember Earle's first visit to the office. Since the staff was in a meeting, he sat down near my desk and we chatted for some time. Earle was very much at ease: natural, open, friendly, and communicative. He was eager to discuss the Fellowship from the perspectives of service, growth, structure, and current events. It was fun that day and on his subsequent visits to share views, news, anecdotes, and opinions on lots of subjects. Besides, he was very handsome, charismatic, and charmed all of us from that day on!

"I don't recall whether or not Earle met Bill on that initial visit, but I think he visited 'Stepping Stones' (Bill and Lois's home in Bedford Hills, New York) several times. They became good friends. Earle was easy to talk with, and liked to share ideas and experiences on many subjects. Bill and Lois enjoyed his kind of conversation, so Earle was always a welcome guest at their home or in New York.

"Perhaps one reason for the close and helpful communication and friendship between Earle and Bill (much appreciated by Bill, I know) was that Bill often found it difficult to discuss his deep, personal feelings with most of his other AA friends. This included Bill's reasons for—and puzzlement over—his long-time depressive periods, and especially aspects of his relationship vis a vis the Fellowship. For example, many AA members held Bill in a kind of saintly awe. Others, while equally grateful and loving, were inclined to describe him—out of his presence —as 'just another drunk.' This was actually one of Bill's own favorite expressions, when he was modestly trying to minimize the effect of too much verbal gratitude from visitors.

"So, to me it was understandable that Bill could relax, could remove the enforced halo, and could confide his feelings and opinions in the unstressful presence of personal nonalcoholic friends—such as Father Ed Dowling, Rev. Dr. Sam Shoemaker, Aldous Huxley, and Gerald Heard—and psychiatrist Dr. Earle M.! All of these and others, at different periods, helped Bill to overcome and dispel for a while a sense of separateness— even a touch of loneliness—that seemed to accompany him as the acknowledged spiritual leader of the AA Fellowship."

Nell Wing, January 1988;
Employed at AA World Services
1947-1982
Secretary to Bill W. 1950-1971

'THE WHISPER OF HUMILITY'

"An article {'The Whisper of Humility' by Earle M.} that does an unsurpassed job of personalizing AA's Twelve Traditions . . ."

AA Grapevine, November 1956

In late 1953, walking back down Lexington Avenue to my Gramercy Park hotel after visiting Bill, his wife Lois, and the New York AA office staff, an idea came to me. Why couldn't the Twelve Traditions* be used as an additional Twelve Steps? If the Traditions were personalized, in my opinion, they would:

1. offer a way to stay sober and a means to maintain sobriety;

2. explain where God was and how to recruit His aid;

3. give the requirements for becoming an AA member;

4. tell how one could maintain one's own autonomy and individuality while being in AA;

5. offer a prime purpose for living: by carrying the message to the alcoholic who still suffered;

6. warn against overinvolvement with prestige, money and outside organizations;

---

*"The Twelve Traditions of AA are suggested principles to ensure the survival and growth of the thousands of groups that make up the fellowship. They are based on the experiences of the groups themselves during the critical early years of the movement." *44 Questions,* AA pamphlet

7. make clear that each AA member is responsible for his own life and sobriety;

8. advise against professionalism within AA;

9. warn against policy of organization;

10. advise avoiding controversy of any sort;

11. make clear that each individual's public relations policy should be based upon attraction, not promotion, and warn against revealing one's identity at the level of press, radio, television and films, lest one get the AA-swelled head and endanger sobriety;

12. state that anonymity was the spiritual foundation of all our traditions, and that our common welfare comes first.

It seemed to me that these personalized traditions offered a way to encourage the growth of humility. When I arrived at my New York hotel, I rushed to my room, pulled out some hotel stationery and wrote for the next three hours. I called my article "The Whisper of Humility."

I was so excited I could hardly wait to deliver my piece to the staff of the Alcoholics Anonymous monthly magazine, the *AA Grapevine.* They were delighted with it and told me it would be published soon. Bill read it and was pleased with the concept of using the Twelve Traditions as an extra Twelve Steps. I left the office and "floated" back to the Gramercy Park hotel quite a distance. I didn't sleep that night because I couldn't get my article out of my mind—I was so excited about having figured out a new concept. The next day, when I had lunch with Lib, Nell, Eve, and Beth, I read my article to them. Bill had already told them about it, and they said they liked it.

That afternoon, I flew to Chicago for a medical meeting. During an AA luncheon at the Palmer House, I met Ed K., who took me to an AA meeting that evening in an Evanston home. The meeting was subdued. There were about twenty people present, mainly men. I shattered the quiet atmosphere with "The Whisper of Humility" story. Although I could see that the group was disturbed by my loud voice and aggressiveness, for the life of me I couldn't stop. They listened patiently. There was a long pause after I finished, and the meeting ended shortly thereafter.

I returned home to San Francisco the next day. Within a few weeks, Ed K. told me that some of the people at the Evanston meeting had thought that I was not "for real." They had contacted Bill W. in New York, who reassured them that I was an AA member in good standing.

My aggressive, hyperactive behavior has made me some enemies over the years, I suppose, but my high spirits and excitement about life have attracted considerably more friends.

"The Whisper of Humility" was first published over three decades ago, in the March 1955 *AA Grapevine*. It has been reprinted several times in that magazine and is in the book *The Best of the Grapevine.*

The Whisper of Humility

"One part of our great program—The Twelve Traditions—has come to mean life itself to me.

"The Traditions, as written by our co-founder Bill, define for me clearly and precisely how to get well and stay well. They tell me who God is, what He does, and where He functions. They show me what spirituality is and how I may seek and find it. They clarify what anonymity means.

"Perhaps most important of all, they point out the path toward humility. It is helpful that this path is not described bluntly; rather it is whispered to me in each Tradition.

"Tradition One tells me that 'Our common welfare should come first . . .' Not second or fourth or tenth, but *first*. Why? Because 'personal recovery depends upon AA unity.' So, I learn that after the Twelve Steps have been digested, my group, my AA, *comes first;* not myself, you understand, but my AA group or groups. My own recovery—my most prized possession, since it means life itself—depends upon my group's unity.

"I am told how to stay well in Tradition One, and to my surprise, it dawns on me that I have received the first gentle whisper which nudges me along the path of humility.

"Tradition Two tells me who God is, where He is, and what He does. It says, 'For our group purpose there is but one ultimate authority . . . a loving God as he may express Himself in our group conscience.' God expresses Himself in a specific location—my conscience. This is good news to me. I have wondered for over forty years where and who God was and what He did. Now I understand what was meant, long ago, by the command, 'Be still and know that I am God.'

"I read on in the last half of Tradition Two and I find the second gentle whisper toward humility: 'Our leaders [you and I] are but trusted servants; they do not govern.' I love the clarity and force of that simple word 'but.' As a leader I *am* but a trusted servant. I need not govern. Thank God! I have been a dubiously trusted leader who felt that he *must* govern for too long; now I may be relieved of all of that. As God may express Himself in my conscience, I am His and your trusted servant, who governs only me.

"Tradition Three tells me that 'The only requirement for AA membership is a desire to stop drinking.' To have a *desire to stop anything* is new to me. So I receive the third gentle whisper toward humility. As I hear and feel these gentle whispers I settle more and more each day to life size, and, as a Los Angeles member has said, 'Life comes to be for free and for fun.'

"Tradition Four brings me clearly and simply into my own right. It says, 'Each group should be autonomous, except in matters affecting other groups or AA as a whole.' You and I are autonomous. Individually and collectively, we may do as we wish, we are unrestricted . . . *except* when we step on someone else's toes or when we step on a group's toes. Thus the fourth gentle whisper toward humility says to me, 'Brother, the common welfare comes first for the truly spiritually selfish reason that your own recovery depends upon its continued existence.'

"Tradition Five defines in clear terms my only reason for existence. There is no other for me: 'Each group has but one primary purpose . . . to carry its message to the alcoholic who still suffers.' There is my answer. I need purpose—and I have it! I must carry the message to the alcoholic who still suffers. So I say to myself, 'Thank God for alcohol and for the unrecovered drunk!' And I hear a fifth gentle whisper toward humility deep within me which says, 'At long last you have come to realize that service to others is all that you have to offer in this life!'

"Tradition Six clarifies the spiritual side of this program. It says, 'An AA group ought never endorse, finance, or lend the AA name to any related facility or outside enterprise lest problems of money, property and prestige divert us from our primary spiritual aim.' I'm glad I know this, because now I can be on guard. I have a primary spiritual aim which money, property and prestige can bust wide open and devour. I hear a sixth gentle whisper toward humility which says, '*Your* primary spiritual aim is to carry the message to the alcoholic who still suffers!' In the role of a trusted servant, I must follow the instructions of a loving authority who lives in the depths of my soul. It says, 'In all reverence carry to the sick alcoholic the message that I have given you.'

"Tradition Seven tells me how to obtain peace of mind. It shows me how to regain my self-respect. At long last I understand the inner peace that comes from being responsible for myself, and to myself. Tradition Seven says, 'Every AA group ought to be fully self-supporting, declining outside contributions.' What relief that is! No longer do I need to *wait* for contributions. I am now free to *give* contributions.

"Tradition Eight gives to me, a professional man, the very keynote of humility: 'Alcoholics Anonymous should remain forever nonprofessional, but our service centers may employ special workers.' I know the professional life; I am in it up to my very ears;

I love it. But I know one other thing, too: in my life of service there is absolutely no room for professionalism. In AA I am an ordinary human being with no more skills than anyone else.

"Tradition Nine astonishes me by stating, 'AA as such ought never be organized; but we may create service boards or committees directly responsible to those they serve.' You see, in the past, I have been so well organized (or so I thought) that I almost died from it! I was frightened at first to find that I needed to be in a group that wasn't organized. But in AA I am free to be myself as I find myself at the minute, and here I find another whisper toward humility: I can be on service boards or committees, and I can be a trusted servant who is directly responsible to you, my fellow AAs.

"Tradition Ten pleases me very much. I read it daily with a joyful smile: 'Alcoholics Anonymous has no opinion on outside issues; hence the AA name ought never be drawn into public controversy.' Just think, as an AA I need never be drawn into public controversy. I don't have to worry about being right. Never again! I don't have to fight anymore. I've had enough of controversy.

"God love our good co-founder, Bill, for taking it easy on my befuddled brain. He held off giving me Tradition Eleven until I could hear and digest Tradition Ten. I read: 'Our public relations policy is based on attraction rather than promotion; we need always maintain personal anonymity at the level of press, radio, and films.'" Never again do I have to promote a single thing . . . I am free to be myself. I am free to believe what I believe. I am free to say what I believe in my own way. And I hear a whisper (number eleven) deep within that says, 'The way to humility is to realize that you *need* to maintain personal anonymity!' It doesn't say that I have to, or that I should, or that I must; it says I *need* to maintain anonymity, as I need the very food and water and air that keeps me alive.

"And so Tradition Twelve comes into view. 'Anonymity is the spiritual foundation of our Traditions, ever reminding us to place principles above personalities.' I've been wondering about this anonymity business. Now I know. Anonymity means that I am only Earle. I am just a guy like you. You and I are equal. I am not a professional man; I am just Earle. The weather way up there on the peak of 'prestige and gain' was bitter cold . . . down here in the world of anonymity, it is warm and balmy. I can shake hands with you and look you straight in the eye and say, 'Hi, my name is Earle.' I am just one guy. No more. No less. I am one of the grains of sand that goes to make up our great beach of AA. Without me as a grain of sand, without each of you as a grain of sand, there would be no AA beach. Without the beach of AA there would be no you and no me.

"So I hear the last and best whisper of all. It says: 'ever reminding us to place principles above personalities.' I smile a deep inward smile. Day after day I come to know that our common welfare comes first, that my God is a living authority located inside of me, that I am His ungoverning, trusted servant who is dedicated to the spiritual activity of carrying the message in complete anonymity to the alcoholic who still suffers.

"I smile because in my organization I am unorganized. I smile because I need not be a professional man who has opinions that he must cram down your throat. I smile because I can at last be myself, and if I don't attract anyone, at least I won't promote anyone.

"But mainly, I smile because you—all of you in AA—have given me the opportunity to fight for your principles rather than my personality."

Earle M., San Francisco,
AA Grapevine, March 1955

I still feel the same way about "The Whisper of Humility" now as I did when I wrote it over thirty years ago. I would not change any of it. I'm very grateful that I felt the urge to write this article, for it still helps *me* today and I hope that it helps other people as well.

Using the Twelve Traditions as Steps actually gives me twelve additional AA Steps. I personalize them: I substitute my name for the AA Program or AA group. For example, Tradition Seven becomes: "*I* ought to be self-supporting, declining outside contributions." To me, this means standing up on my own two feet not only financially but in *every* area of my life.

I Planned to 'Resign' from AA

"You join AA by going to meetings. You quit by taking a drink."

Paul H., *Things My Sponsor Taught Me*

During that first year of sobriety (1953–54), I was on fire with AA activity and my new religious leanings. I was on the phone constantly: with Jack I., secretary of the San Francisco Central AA Fellowship; with Paul G., a later secretary of that office; and with Stan W., California's first delegate to the General Service Conference in New York.

However, one Sunday morning I felt upset and disenchanted with my AA life. Perhaps I had been paying too much attention to the Jesus as Teacher group, and too little to AA. (In my opinion, somewhere between three and six months of sobriety, the presence of a lingering physical toxicity—especially from alcohol—can manifest itself in a feeling of disenchantment with a sober way of life and all that it entails.)

I went to a Sunday morning AA meeting in San Rafael, Marin County, specifically to announce that I planned to "resign" from AA. I had experienced low emotional periods in my early sobriety, but this one—occurring out of the blue, completely unexpectedly—was the worst.

Olive E., who greeted all AA members at the door, asked me what was wrong. I blurted that I had decided to resign from AA because I felt so miserable. Olive, a wise AA veteran, later told me that she didn't attempt to reason with me or try to talk me out of my decision, because my agitation was too great. She merely said, in a friendly way, "Well, as long as you're here, why don't you attend the meeting? You can resign when it's over."

At that meeting, just as in many AA meetings all over the world, the Big Book and *Twelve Steps and Twelve Traditions* were raffled off. To my surprise, *I* won the Big Book! Since I already owned several copies, I gave it to a newcomer—and that made me feel better.

The meeting began after the raffle. Chuck C., the speaker, had a Kentucky twang. He laughed raucously and frequently at himself. He was large-boned, handsome, immaculately dressed, and seemed to be in touch with something that I wanted.

I had heard many AA speakers, but none as exciting as Chuck. As I listened, my anger and agitation gradually subsided. I became entranced with him. The tone and intensity of his presentation were ministerial. His use of biblical and religious terms were colloquial. For example, he substituted "the young carpenter from Nazareth" for the name "Jesus." In his drinking days, he had been called "the drunken deacon." Now he was a sober deacon! Chuck spoke for an hour that morning and nearly carried me into the Kingdom of Heaven. I was amazed, awestruck, and instantly devoted to this marvelous man.

After the meeting, some of us went to a gathering at Thelma H.'s house in Tiburon. Chuck and I spent a couple of hours talking, and my enchantment with him intensified.

I decided not to resign from AA.

Soon after that, I met Chuck's wife, Elsa, and his two sons. I visited Chuck's home in southern California many times. I loved talking with Chuck, but as the years passed I became increasingly uncomfortable with the friendship. My brand of AA developed in ways that differed from his in many respects. I felt as if I couldn't believe him, and would wonder, Is he for real? I realized that I could not follow his path. For better or for worse, I felt that I must hone out an AA way of life that appealed and applied to me. This was very painful. Chuck and I slowly drifted apart. We remained basically devoted, however, and when he died in December 1984,

I grieved deeply. He was a major influence in my early sobriety and I miss him.

Looking back on those early AA days, I can see today that a sense of irritability over some things about "traditional AA" was beginning to creep into my consciousness. In this case, traditional AA refers to members whom I considered to be religionists, and who emphasized God with what appeared to me to be a bias.

Frank B. and the Seven Seas Club

Another important person in my early AA years was Frank B. Born on skid row, both parents alcoholic, Frank grew up by his fists and the seat of his pants. He spent most of his life on the San Francisco waterfront, though he managed to finish high school, and he even attended Cornell University for a few months.

Frank had been a merchant marine. When World War II started, he was inducted into the Navy and assigned to the Pacific Coast Fleet. He was dependable aboard ship, but on leave and on shore it was a different story: Frank was a hard, two-fisted drinker—a drunken, fighting terror.

He hit San Francisco's skid row after the war—a drunk, and he knew it.

One day Frank decided to sober up and join AA. So, with a coffee pot and the Big Book, he started the Seven Seas Club at 9 Mission Street. The Club became a gathering place for maritime skid row alcoholics.

When I came into AA, Frank and the Seven Seas Club housed and fed about twenty-five recovering skid row maritime drunks. Clark B., the butcher from my Mill Valley AA group, supplied meat at cost to Frank.

I had read a suggestion in an AA pamphlet that one do something each day for someone, but do it in secrecy. If one was discovered, the act of kindness did not "count." This was supposed to teach the importance of anonymity in service. The concept appealed to me, and I tried to do little things every day that I hoped would help people. Happily I was never discovered, and one reward was the indescribable emotional high that would follow each act.

One day I wondered if Frank needed a freezer in which to store the meat he got from Clark. I phoned him (I had not yet met him, only heard about him) and said, "I'm a new member of AA, and I understand that you buy meat from Clark for the Club."

He said, "I get yah. Who's this?"

"I'd just as soon not say," I replied. "But I wondered if you could use a deep-freeze?"

Frank paused. "Yah. We've saved around two hundred bucks. Maybe we'll have enough for one next year."

"If I sent you one now, could you use it?"

"Sure could," Frank said. "Who's this?" When I refused to tell him, he said, "Oh, you're doing one of those things to not get found out. That it?" And then told me he understood.

That very day, I paid cash to a wholesaler for a large freezer and had it sent to the Seven Seas Club. I lingered in my parked car outside my house that evening, caught up in the ecstasy of my secret deed. I felt an overpowering sensation of love, gentle but intense. I had not experienced such a feeling since my spiritual awakening on the last day of my drinking.

Three days later I phoned Frank to see if the freezer had arrived. He expressed his appreciation. I hung up without disclosing who I was, and once again felt ecstatic.

Then I got greedy. I wanted more and more of that great feeling. I called Frank to see if he could use some cash to buy more meat. He said he could, again asked my name, and again I refused to divulge it. That afternoon I put three hundred-dollar bills in an envelope with a note: "I hope this will be of some value to you and the members of the Club."

A few days later, when I phoned Frank, he told me that the money had arrived. He thanked me and I felt high, but I sensed that I had pushed my luck.

I finally met Frank about eight months later. I still did not reveal our prior relationship, because the whole idea had been based on maintaining my anonymity.

A week after that, Frank came to our Mill Valley meeting with some members of the Seven Seas Club. After the meeting, he said that he must hurry back to the Club. One of his boys was sick with bronchitis and needed to be taken to a nearby hospital. I told Frank that I'd be glad to write a prescription for penicillin, which would save him a trip.

Two weeks later, Frank showed up again at the Mill Valley meeting. "Hey, buddy, aren't you the guy that sent us the deep-freeze and dough for meat?" he asked me.

Feigning ignorance, I said I had no idea what he was talking about. Then Frank showed me two pieces of paper: the anonymous note I had sent with the three hundred dollars, and my penicillin prescription, which he had not used. "Look, the handwriting is the same," he said.

I was flustered. But Frank looked at me in such a way that I realized I had been "caught." I admitted I was the donor, but said that I'd wanted to keep it anonymous.

"I understand," he said. "It's a noble thing to do. But just as you gotta keep this a secret, we at the Club gotta say thank you."

I spent a good deal of time at the Seven Seas Club in the ensuing years and became very friendly with Frank and his boys. Every time I passed the freezer, my memory went back to the glorious days when I did something for someone anonymously. Later I donated twenty-five beds and large amounts of vitamins to the club, but I never again felt the emotional thrill I'd had over that anonymous deep-freeze gift.

Frank cannot be adequately described. It's necessary to spend hours with him in order to see and to know his greatness. Frank talks in jerky phrases. His conversations seem unintelligible, but when he *says* things, you instantly understand. He is a deeply devoted, earnest, and courageous man. He never wastes anyone's time, and people trust him completely. Though Frank is rough and tough, he stands out as a shining example of good AA. Frank recently celebrated his forty-second anniversary in the Program.

PIGEONS REPLACE PARTYING

". . . Some of us find we can't think up non-drinking things to do! Perhaps this is because we're just out of the habit. Or perhaps the mind needs a period of restful convalescence after active alcoholism ceases. In either case, the dullness goes away. . . ."

Living Sober

After my physical recovery was virtually complete, I had emotional problems adjusting to life without the aid of alcohol and drugs. One problem was the weekends. I simply did not know what to do with myself. In the past, I'd filled my weekends with drinking and partying. Now that I was sober, the weekends hung heavy: dark, dank, awesome, lonely. It was sheer drudgery to live through the hours. A Sunday morning AA meeting helped a great deal, but I felt lost the rest of the time.

I had no idea how to relieve this discomfort. For a while, I simply lived with it.

Then one day my eleven-year-old daughter, Jane, announced with great excitement that a boy in her class at school was going to give her "a couple of pigeons." She planned to bring them home the next day.

I recoiled and said sternly, "We have dogs, cats, a horse, hamsters, and so forth. That's enough. Pigeons are out!"

My daughter gave me a short dissertation on the value of racing pigeons. I was spellbound by her enthusiasm, sweetness, and childlike logic. But I wanted to be adamant. I said, "If there are any pigeons around here, they'll have to be a long, long way from this house." Meaning, for example, the North Pole.

The next evening, when I came home, Jane had dug a four-by-six-foot level area in the side of the hill, twenty feet from the house. She was still working when I approached.

"What are you doing?" I asked irritably.

"Well, you said that if we had pigeons, they'd have to be a long way from the house, and I figured that this is pretty far," she said.

What does a father do in a situation like this? I didn't feel wise or clever, so I restated my original position: "There'll be no pigeons around here. You have enough animals."

During dinner Jane again regaled me with the value of racing pigeons. Her enthusiasm was lovable, infectious, and beautiful, but I was determined not to be budged.

By the next evening, she'd taken some of my best redwood lumber to build a four-foot-square box. I'd planned to use that lumber elsewhere. "I guess you're wondering what I'm doing?" she said. "Well, I'm making a box for the pigeons."

Rather archly, I said, "Jane, there will be no pigeons around here. I want you to hear that!" But Jane was not to be stopped, nor her enthusiasm squashed. That night at dinner, she again gave me the pitch on the value of racing pigeons. I listened intently, unimpressed! But her drive to accomplish something *did* impress me.

Well, I thought, if racing pigeons means that much to her, I'd better do something about it. The next weekend, Janey and I visited Jack Varney of our local hardware store, who gave me the name of a racing pigeon fancier on the West Rim of Mill Valley. He showed Janey and me around his loft, then opened the trap door and a flock of thirty pigeons flew out. As I watched them circle over Mill Valley, I became as enthusiastic as my daughter about the sport.

Jane and I went home and discussed where to put a pigeon loft and where to secure the birds. She was most willing to work. We drove to the local lumber yard and ordered lumber, cement blocks, nails, wire, and all the necessary accoutrements to build a pigeon loft. I was not an accomplished carpenter, but I was so determined to try building a loft that I arranged to leave my office for two weeks in order to try. My daughter helped after school and on weekends. I had never built anything like this, and I was rather pleased with the results. So was Janey.

This project is a good example of how an AA parent can try to relate to his or her child.

We joined the local pigeon club. Some members gave us a few baby pigeons to raise. I bought more from local breeders, and later even went all the way to Pennsylvania to buy racing pigeons. Before long, Jane and I were in the pigeon business. We began training our birds to race. Now my weekends were filled with activity and enthusiasm, rather than with lassitude and depression. An age-old statement in *Alcoholics Anonymous* says, "If you stay sober, good things are bound to happen." This pigeon project with Janey is a prime example.

Jane and I even won a couple of races! Janey clocked in the winning pigeons, and since she'd instigated the whole business, she deserved to win.

We continued in the pigeon business until Jane graduated from high school in 1959. Then she went off to the Academy of Music at Oberlin College. I raced the pigeons alone for a couple of years, but it just wasn't the same without Janey. Soon I realized that the birds had served their purpose. We had reached the end of a phase.

I kept the pigeons as pets for about two months, until a friend from the pigeon club said, "It's too bad you keep those pigeons locked up all the time. They're racers. They're athletes. They should be exercised and utilized."

I gave him all the pigeons. He was delighted. I visited him from time to time, to look over my old friends. He bred winners from that group but, of course, he couldn't release them from his loft (unless they were sitting on eggs, which could be all the time) because they would have flown back to my loft. Pigeons are that way.

To this day, I am deeply grateful for my daughter's childish enthusiasm about pigeons. And I am grateful to the pigeons. They filled my drab weekends with zest, and they brought me and Janey closer together.

Sobriety offered many happy occurrences for me. The two often go hand in hand in AA.

A daughter looks back

▲ ▲ ▲ ▲ ▲ ▲ ▲ ▲ ▲

"I'm told that my father seemed to drink seven times as much as most people. People would think he'd had just a couple of drinks, but he'd really have a lot more and slowly fall asleep. I was a very little girl then, but I believe this. He's always been an extremist.

"You could say that my father had a personality change when he drank: he was the life of the party. *Nobody* was more fun! He changed when he stopped drinking: that brought out a very serious side. Less humor. I think that he's stayed this way through the other changes in his life.

"I didn't know about it when he stopped drinking, even though I was with him at Sam's Restaurant the morning that he had his last drink. He told my mother he was an alcoholic and that he was going to AA. She was as supportive as she could be then; she didn't drink for a year in an effort to help him. I was an intuitive kid—I knew something was up. He finally did tell me that he was a recovering alcoholic, but he didn't tell his patients until he felt 'on top of it' more. I think he was concerned that people would reprimand him professionally for being an alcoholic. He's since gone down in AA's history with his story in the Big Book. As a speaker, he's helped people too. He's a very volcanic person. Not easy to understand, and not to be underestimated. . . ."

Jane M., Dr. Earle's daughter

SOBER ON STAGE

"My father always loved to perform."

Jane M., Dr. Earle's daughter

The magic of theater has always fascinated me. I directed and performed in regional theater during high school, college, and even medical school. I always had a rather presentable singing voice, so I did some professional singing as a student.

My first wife, Mary, had majored in drama at Stanford University. During my first year of sobriety, she took up acting again with a local amateur theatrical group. During my second year of sobriety, Mary suggested that I direct William Inge's *Come Back, Little Sheba* (about an alcoholic chiropractor and his wife), since AA had a role in the play. I'd always enjoyed directing and I was intrigued by Inge's view of sobriety as being drab and lonely. I cast and rehearsed the play, which ran for several months. Mary was most convincing in the lead. (After all, she'd had experience with an active, and now recovering, alcoholic!)

Racing pigeons filled my previously empty weekend days. Now amateur theater filled many of my evenings. But I was still close to the Program, for most of the backstage crew were AA members.

I read plays continually. One that especially interested me was *Inherit the Wind,* in which characters representing lawyers William Jennings Bryan and Clarence S. Darrow cross swords at the 1925 trial of John T. Scopes, who was arrested for teaching evolution in Tennessee public schools, contrary to state law. In the closing scene, Clarence Darrow ("Drummond" in the play, and Scopes' attorney) holds up a Bible alongside Darwin's *The Origin of the Species,* which represents science. Clarence Darrow gently places the books together, implying that religion and science are up to the same thing. This gesture underscored *my* feeling about religion and science: that each approaches the same thing from a different point of view.

I directed *Inherit the Wind.* I selected the cast of sixty, directed rehearsals, and acted the part of Drummond. Mary played William Jennings Bryan's wife beautifully. The play ran successfully for four months. Performances were Thursday through Sunday evenings, which left three nights (and every day) free for AA meetings.

In the past, my drinking and medical practice had taken me away from home. Now, in my sobriety, theater contributed to my absence from home. I left the Mill Valley theater scene and joined other theatrical groups—in Sausalito, Tiburon, and San Francisco. These groups were more sophistocated than Mill Valley's; the men and women had solid experience in theater, and made an avocation of it. Mary was not interested in joining me, saying she felt responsible for our home, our daughter, her two sisters, and her mother. But although Mary abandoned acting, she did attend dress rehearsals and performances of all the plays and musicals that I directed. She was a good critic; I valued her suggestions.

In 1964, sober eleven years, I cast and directed my final play, Friedrich Dürrenmatt's *The Deadly Game.* The play received that year's award for best amateur performance in the San Francisco Bay Area.

I still don't know why, but the urge to do more theater left me after *The Deadly Game.* I had invested heavily in equipment—lights, dimmer boards, recording equipment, and mixers—all of which I sold at a low price to the Mill Valley Center for the Performing Arts. I've always thought that I didn't give up alcohol—rather, alcohol gave me up. The same was true with theater. I didn't leave it—theater left me. So did smoking cigarettes in 1967 after I struggled for years to stop a four-pack-a-day addiction.

Perhaps people go through cycles which come to an end. My interest in theater is still there, but the urge to be actively involved has disappeared. The craving to do more theater, like the craving to drink, vanished years ago and has never reappeared.

My Father and I and AA

"Periodic Alcoholism: alcoholism in which bouts of gross drinking alternate with long periods of abstinence or moderation."

A Dictionary of Words about Alcohol

Alcoholics Anonymous brought my father and me together. My dad was a good father when I was a kid—a periodic alcoholic who never drank or raised hell at home, nor did he deny his drinking problem. When the police or health department would call and I had to go bring him home, there was no feeling of shame or stigma about it. I always knew I could go to him about anything—he was tender, and available to his kids.

My dad stopped drinking by himself in about 1933, shortly before the founding of AA. He stayed sober for twelve years, until V-J Day, the final day of World War II, when he took one drink. That drink led to a three-day alcoholic binge, and he ended up in the hospital, bleeding from the stomach and the rectum. He was given eight blood transfusions. After he recovered, he never drank again.

My father was a classic example of the alcoholic, who cannot safely take one single drink. When I was a child, he used to tell me that he could stay sober as long as he *didn't take that first drink*. On V-J Day, he forgot. Some alcoholics do. I'm grateful that I never have.

My AA membership intrigued my father. He read the Big Book avidly, and liked it. However he did not join AA because, he said, except for the V-J bender in 1945 he'd been sober for over twenty years. He did attend a few AA meetings, if I was chairman or if I gave a talk, but mainly he came to observe his son.

Though my father stayed sober without benefit of help, he was not especially happy. My mother never stopped drinking, and they never divorced. Her alcoholism was mild and progressed very slowly.

After I joined AA in 1953, however, and my dad became acquainted with the Program through me, a peacefulness settled over him. When he would tell me about his own drinking career, I would feel almost as if we were having an AA meeting. My membership in Alcoholics Anonymous drew us close, and I shall ever be grateful for that.

My father died in 1957 after a six-month illness. He had been a Blue Lodge Mason. During his Masonic burial, I had a sudden urge to become a Mason. Clark, from my Mill Valley AA group, was a Mason, and he helped get me admitted to the Mill Valley Masonic Lodge. He schooled me in the Masonic traditions and taught me the first Three Degrees of Masonry. I became a Blue Lodge member.

By now four years sober, I was beginning to feel a sense of separation from religion. I had redefined God as I understood Him. I was slowly entering the Irritable phase of my AA life. Although I was deeply spiritual, the religious aspects of Masonry escaped me. Their rituals and rules were incompatible with what I believed. I had a warm, almost sacred feeling for the Masons but, after taking my Third Degree in Masonry, I asked for release from my membership and I never returned.

ANYWHERE, ANYPLACE, ANYTIME

*"I am responsible . . . when anyone, anywhere, reaches out for help, I
want the hand of A.A. always to be there. And for that I am responsible."*

Declaration of Thirtieth Anniversary,
AA International Convention, 1965

In early 1954, shortly after my eighth month of sobriety, I was
asked to "speak" at an AA meeting in Oakland, across the Bay from
San Francisco. As a physician, I had done a good deal of public
speaking about medicine. This, however, was my first time to
"speak" in AA. I accepted eagerly. That evening someone asked me
if I felt apprehensive about addressing the meeting, since I was a
physician and my medical reputation might be endangered. I said,
"I'll talk anyway, even if *all* my patients come to the meeting."
None of them did. The important point was that it made no difference to me. I had decided that if any patient left my care because
I was a sober alcoholic, then it was time for that patient to leave.
To my knowledge, I never lost a patient because I was a recovered
alcoholic!

And then it happened: speaking ignited a flame. Beginning
that evening in 1954 and for many years thereafter, I accepted all
invitations to speak at AA functions. Anywhere. Anyplace. Any-
time. I was "on fire" about AA and what it had done for me.

I fell in love with my own voice. I emoted and cried as I related
my AA story. I'd always been a ham—an actor—and here were
countless stages just waiting for me! I cringe now at the memory

of my emotional antics. I painted myself as a Latter Day Christ in Alcoholics Anonymous. And although my talks reeked with self-pity, I hope now that, in spite of this, I got my message across.

I stayed on the AA lecture circuit for a good decade, until one day I sickened of my voice. In the early 1960s, I was speaking at an AA convention in Louisiana. In the middle of my talk I became painfully aware that what I was saying had lost its freshness. For the first time, I saw clearly that I'd smothered my presentations in needless emotion, tears, and self-pity. Perhaps I had been trying too hard to emulate Chuck C. and others. At that point I decided to decrease my AA speaking engagements. I began to refuse invitations, and within a few years they grew sparse. I became more interested in my own AA group than in showing off on the AA lecture platform.

But my sense of loss with my AA talks was temporarily neutralized by meeting Joe L., a wonderful AA member from Tyler, Texas. Joe is one of the funniest men I've known. When in doubt, or in need of a lift, I could always call Joe. He knew just what to say to me to make me feel better. More important: regardless of my mood, he was always my friend.

THE BLACKBOARD TALK

"Heavy drinking is initiated by psychological or social factors; later a physiological X factor accounts for a disease condition outwardly manifested through loss of control."

Theory formulated by Jellinek, 1945-1953,
and expressed in **E. M. Jellinek,** *The Disease Concept of Alcoholism*

". . . The alcoholic has within him a trigger mechanism known as the x-factor or tendency to develop the disease of alcoholism, thought by some to be present within him from birth. The x-factor probably includes a variety of physical, emotional, and spiritual elements, but it seems to be primarily a physical thing.

Because of the presence of the x-factor the alcoholic-to-be becomes a different person when alcohol is taken into his body. He steps onto the road to alcoholism with his first drink. His tolerance to and need for alcohol increase constantly and his battle for social approval becomes more discouraging. He becomes vicitimized by a true physiological process. Once the disease has started it never stops as long as the alcoholic continues to drink. It is always progressive. It can never be cured. But it can be arrested. The treatment is sobriety, with some change in the manner of living."

Dr. Earle M., "Here's Why,"
AA Grapevine, April 1959

In the mid-1950s, during my lecture circuit phase, I met Robert Gordon Bell, M.D., a nonalcoholic who directed an alcohol treatment center in Canada. When we discussed the medical factors in alcoholism, we found we both believed that there must be a physical component in alcoholism.

At that time, most physicians still felt that alcoholism was symptomatic of some underlying psychological deficit. Both Dr. Bell and I had seen many patients with intense emotional problems that easily overshadowed those of the average alcoholic. These people could drink or not as they saw fit . . . but not so the alcoholic. Why was this? we wondered.

We both suspected that there must be *something physical* within the alcoholic which, when *combined with alcohol, creates alcoholism; that alcoholic emotions and behavior* arise *from the alcoholic's drinking, rather than being the cause of the drinking.*

This theory launched me on more than three decades of educational lecturing about alcoholism—I called it "The Blackboard Talk"—which continues to this day.

In 1959 I wrote an article for the *AA Grapevine* about the x-factor (the unknown physical principle) in the alcoholic. I described what I saw as seven physical differences between alcoholics and nonalcoholics:

1. *"Hyperinsulinism* [now known as *hypoglycemia*]:

   "When a simple sugar is taken into the alcoholic's body his blood sugar increases. Immediately his pancreas is stimulated to secrete excessive amounts of insulin and within a half an hour to an hour his blood sugar drops to a very low level. This phenomenon seems to be true whether or not he is an active (drinking) alcoholic or an inactive (sober) alcoholic.

   "The symptoms of low blood sugar state are: tremulousness, depression, headache, bloating, muscle tension, sense of dissatisfaction, irritability, uncooperativeness, sweating, and insomnia, to mention a few. Perhaps this is why a shot of alcohol [a sugar] is so appealing to the alcoholic. As his blood sugar level increases, a sense of well-being comes over him. He is at peace once again physically, emotionally and spiritually (or so he believes)."

". . . the body of the alcoholic seems to utilize sugar in exactly the same way irrespective of drunkenness or sobriety.
While drinking his choice of sugar is different, that's all!"

2. *"Hypotension:*

". . . low blood pressure levels seem to be more common in
the [sober] alcoholic than in the non-alcoholic. [However, in
early recovery hypertension is usually present.] This is especially true in the morning or after long periods of loafing.
The symptoms of hypotension are depression, dizziness, list-
lessness, irritability, quick anger, fullness in the head, swell-
ing of face, hands and feet, sense of oppression, a deep sense
of fatigue, a hatred for being alive and a 'hangdog'
expression—again to mention only a few.

". . . some food and a little exercise . . . do wonders for that
'off the [AA] Program' feeling."

3. "Some authorities believe that *oxygen tension in the brain* of
the alcoholic is lower than in the non-alcoholic. How this
adds to the alcoholic's irritability!"

4. "The alcoholic's *requirement for fluids* is fantastic. [As time
goes by, this seems to subside in many.] He downs buckets
of coffee, water, juices, etc., as the non-alcoholic looks on in
dumb amazement at this injudicious slurping."

5. *"Increased muscle tension* has been observed by kymograph
readings in both the active and sober alcoholic. [This tension
tends to subside over time.] Apparently the alcoholic is a
tense bird [most are, anyway] and must live with it forever
more."

6. "The alcoholic is [often] *restless, active, irritable and on the
constant go.* He seems driven by an unseen force. When the
alcoholic decides to act he can be a whirlwind . . . Incidentally, there are many times when he doesn't relish activity and

can be found flat on his back contemplating God knows what!
What a tough guy to live with!"

7. "Oddly enough, there is a *lowered incidence of obesity and baldness* among alcoholics than is to be found in the population as a whole. Why? No one knows . . . ."

Dr. Earle M., "Here's Why," *AA Grapevine,* April 1959

Since this *Grapevine* article was published, a great deal of scientific research has provided a clearer description of the physical nature of addiction. I continually add current scientific findings to my Blackboard Talk.

Thirty years after I wrote "Here's Why," I would change little. (Minor changes are shown in brackets in the reprinted article.) Some would disagree with me. But the article, correct or incorrect, represents an honest groping on my part for those factors which I believe lead to and/or signal addiction.

Today, most authorities (although not all) agree that an important factor in alcoholism is genetics: familial susceptibility or predisposition to the disease.

Research in the last ten years indicates that chemical addictions share many traits despite the drugs used—alcohol, heroin, barbiturates, marijuana, cocaine, benzodiazepines, and others. One day we may find that "an addiction is an addiction is an addiction."

WE STOPPED IN TIME

"Among today's {1955} incoming AA members, many have never reached the advanced stages of alcoholism, though, given time, all might have.

Most of these fortunate ones have had little or no acquaintance with delirium, with hospitals, asylums, and jails. . . .

. . . these seventeen AA's and hundreds of thousands like them, have been saved years of infinite suffering. They sum it up like this: 'We didn't wait to hit bottom because, thank God, we could see the bottom. Actually, the bottom came up and hit us. That sold us on Alcoholics Anonymous.' "

Alcoholics Anonymous, Second Edition

The first annual Folsom Prison (in California) AA convention in 1954 was an especially important one for me. A tape of my talk there was sent to Bill W. He suggested that my story be included in the Second Edition of the Big Book, in the section "They Stopped in Time," along with eleven other so-called "high bottom" stories. I was very flattered and I made several trips to New York to work with Bill, his secretary Nell Wing, and Ed, who was the editor of this revised edition. Not many corrections were necessary, but I always looked for any excuse to see my New York AA friends.

I still consider it a signal honor that my story, called "Physician, Heal Thyself," is included in *Alcoholics Anonymous,* beginning with that Second Edition which was published in 1955 (see page xxvii).

My hope was, and still is, that my story will help others to see the alcoholic handwriting on the wall, and to stop using alcohol and/or other drugs before disaster strikes. Over the years, I've discussed early alcoholism and other drug addiction with many new AA members. I can relate easily to them. Some stay sober. Some don't. Some have progressed to a lower alcoholic bottom, but fortunately some of these have come back and sobered up in the Program.

AA Comes of Age

"During the first three days of July, 1955, Alcoholics Anonymous held a Convention in St. Louis, commemorating the twentieth anniversary of its founding. There our Fellowship declared itself come to the age of full responsibility, and there it received from its founders and old-timers permanent keeping of its three great legacies of Recovery, Unity, and Service . . . .

". . . the testimony of Dr. Earle M., the A.A. member of the panel. A notable in medical circles from coast to coast, Dr. Earle flatly stated that despite his medical knowledge, which included psychiatry, he had nevertheless been obliged humbly to learn his A.A. from a butcher. Thus he confirmed all that Dr. Harry {Tiebout} had told us about the necessity of reducing the alcoholic's ballooning ego, before entering A.A. and afterward."

Alcoholics Anonymous Comes of Age

The Alcoholics Anonymous Twentieth Anniversary Convention was held in St. Louis in 1955. This convention was a momentous occasion in the history of AA. There, on July 3, Bill W. withdrew as formal leader of AA. He turned AA over to its membership, represented by the General Service Conference. AA's Board of Trustees would now be directly accountable to this General Service Conference.

For years Bill had devoted his time to the organization of these two governing groups. He knew, in all wisdom, that he and co-founder Dr. Bob were expendable, and that some sort of structure would be needed to steer the AA ship. Bill formulated the General Service Conference on the principles of the U.S. Senate and House of Representatives: about ninety-five delegates, representing grassroots AA members from all sections of the AA world, would meet every spring. Bill's plan was for this General Service Conference to "take its affairs into its own hands" and "become the permanent successor to the founders of Alcoholics Anonymous."

Bill had trouble selling the idea of the General Service Conference to the AA membership. People feared that the system would be too far removed from the average AA member. They were wrong. The Conference *could* reach each member, through area representatives meeting annually in New York.

Bill "turned over AA to the 'drunks' " at 4:00 P.M. on the final day of that 1955 international convention. On stage were representatives of the General Service Conference and the AA Board of Trustees, plus many other dignitaries, including Bill's wife and his mother.

The Kiel Auditorium was tightly packed with twelve or thirteen thousand people. The weather was kind of hot and we had only minimal air conditioning, but we were too excited to care. I sat near the stage, with Ebby T. on my left and Chuck C. and his wife, Elsa, (of Beverly Hills and, later, Laguna Beach) on my right. The mood was high; everyone felt fifteen or sixteen feet off the ground. After all, this was a moment to remember—Bill W. turning AA over to the drunks!

The afternoon was highly emotional. There wasn't a dry eye in the house. Texan Icky S., the first recovering alcoholic to be a member of the AA Board of Trustees, was master of ceremonies.

Icky told the following story in his rich Texas twang:

"In East Texas, there was a little town with no place to house a drunk. It was agreed that if a drunk appeared on the scene, he should be kept in the local ice house. One finally did come along, and sure enough, according to plan, he was placed in the ice house.

"That evening at dinner the sheriff suddenly realized that the alcoholic in the ice house had been forgotten. He jumped up and told

his wife that he had to go quickly to the ice house and let the fellow out, lest he freeze. The sheriff put on his hat, hurried down the street to the little green ice house, and pulled on the big handle. The door squeaked open, and a ray of light crept into the room.

"In a far corner was a little drunk, all huddled up, who screamed at the sheriff, 'For God's sake, close that door. I'm freezing to death!' "

Icky's story brought down the house.

After explaining the purpose of the AA General Service Conference and the AA Board of Trustees, with one magnificently dignified gesture, AA's co-founder Bill W. turned the workings of Alcoholics Anonymous over to the members of the Conference and the Board, who were on stage.

The applause was deafening. We gave Bill and the newly formed Conference and Board a ten-minute standing ovation. I remember crying like a baby. I believed that God had joined us in the Kiel Auditorium that evening.

So many events of that convention are etched in my memory. Bernard B. Smith, nonalcoholic chairman of the Board of AA, gave a fabulous talk on the First Step of AA. He said that as the alcoholic admits total powerlessness over alcohol, he paradoxically is offered a new kind of power: sobriety. I had never thought about it that way before. I recall Nell Wing, Bill's secretary, prancing around the convention like an excited fairy. She was the mistress of good will.

I was a speaker with two other physicians, Harry M. Tiebout, M.D., and Marvin Block, M.D. I told my story. I also introduced W. W. Bauer, M.D., of the American Medical Association. He praised AA's growing role in the recovery from alcoholism from a medical point of view. Dr. Tiebout, who had been Bill's psychiatrist in the mid-1940s, talked about "ego reduction"—surrender in sobriety. Dr. Block described some of the medical facets of alcoholism that were known at that time. I was excited and deeply honored to be included with these and other greats.

In the audience was Father Edward Dowling, S.J., the little Jesuit priest who gave so much comfort to Bill. And Ebby T., who brought the message of sobriety to Bill. And the Reverend Canon Samuel H. Shoemaker, D.D., Oxford Movement minister who had converted Ebby. And Sister Ignatia, the tiny Catholic sister and nurse, who helped Dr. Bob set up the country's first alcohol unit in Akron. She was as big as a minute, quick on her feet, nimble in her thinking, and devoted to the AA Program.

Ebby, who had difficulty staying sober, had very little money to live on. Bill, in all of his kindness, arranged with some AA friends to give Ebby a lifetime income of about two hundred dollars a month. In those days, that was quite a sum. Ebby moved to Texas, under Icky S.'s observation and protection. He stayed sober for the last five or six years of his life. In addition to alcohol, Ebby had been addicted to other drugs; he and I exchanged a good number of letters concerning drug and alcohol addiction. Ebby was small of stature, but big in mood and ideation. Unfortunately, he carried a resentment toward Bill: Bill had formed AA; Ebby had failed to do so. Bill was aware of this resentment, so he always introduced Ebby as his sponsor, and remained grateful to Ebby for bringing him the message of sobriety.

I was fortunate to become a good friend of these people, who were so very important and vital to the history of AA. My AA life was deeply enriched by friendships of this kind.

'PROK' KINSEY AND
HIS SEXUALITY RESEARCH

"Although he {Dr. Kinsey} cared nothing about drinking for its own sake, or for the effects of alcohol, he became a collector of drink recipes, had an excellent bar built into his home, and was able to make from it an almost professional selection."

Wardell B. Pomeroy, Ph.D.,
Dr. Kinsey and the Institute for Sex Research

In 1946, before I stopped drinking, I met Alfred C. Kinsey, Sc.D., in New York City through Robert Latou Dickinson, M.D. Bobby Dickinson, then eighty-four, was a great master in the gynecological field. Coincidentally, Marty Mann's office at the National Council on Alcoholism was right above Bobby Dickinson's office at the New York Academy of Sciences—but I wouldn't be meeting Marty for quite a few years. Kinsey was a biology professor at Indiana University in Bloomington, well known in zoology circles for his studies of the gall wasp. He also taught a marriage course.

Affectionately known as "Prok," Kinsey was one of the kindest, most fatherly men I have ever known. His students frequently sought his advice about sexual matters. Kinsey was disturbed by his inability to answer many of their questions. Eventually he decided that the best way to find these answers would be to actually ask people how they conducted their sex lives. He correctly surmised that a cross-section of male and female sexual activity could be collected and compiled as a basis for understanding human sexual behavior.

To accomplish this research, Kinsey relinquished his duties as biology professor, though he remained on the Indiana University faculty and drew a meager salary.

In 1947 he founded the Institute for Sexual Research at Indiana University.

Kinsey and I became friends right away. The fact that I was an obstetrician/gynecologist as well as a psychiatrist/marriage counselor interested him. He later told me that he was particularly impressed by my non-punitive sexual outlook and attitudes, for he believed that preconceived sexual opinions, ideals, and concepts were a gross handicap in the field of sex research.

In the late 1940s, he invited me to become a gynecological consultant to the research for his study: *Sexual Behavior in the Human Female.* (This book was published in 1953. Kinsey's first book, *Sexual Behavior in the Human Male,* was published in 1948. The two books became known as *The Kinsey Report.*)

My research took place in Bloomington and in San Francisco. I visited the Indiana University campus frequently, where Prok and his wife, Mac, kindly invited me to stay at their home.

Prok was a true scholar, knowledgeable in many fields including music and electronics—particularly the new hi-fi phonographic equipment of that time. He had a large collection of classical records, and he knew them well. He knew when a composition had been recorded, the conductor's name, why he conducted in a specific fashion, and the composition's history. On Sunday evenings, professors from various fields—astronomy, English, mathematics, biology—gathered in the Kinsey living room for record concerts. In an interesting and gentle fashion, Prok would talk for a few minutes on the origin, composer, and recording of each piece.

At this time I was approaching—but had not yet reached—the end of my drinking days. The Kinseys would offer visitors a glass of wine to sip throughout the evening. My alcohol requirements were too high for that, and anyway, wine didn't appeal to me. Being a generous person, Kinsey laid in a supply of vodka and bourbon for me. Unhappily, I usually drank too much and became rather obnoxious. This was absolutely unindicated at academic gatherings of this sort, but Kinsey did not criticize me for my behavior. He was a totally accepting person.

During my fourth month of sobriety, I visited Prok, Mac, and the Institute for Sex Research staff in Bloomington. Prok invited me to his home for a barbecue dinner for his family and staff. Once the party got under way, I noted Prok going to great lengths to shield me from the wine and other alcoholic beverages being consumed in normal amounts by others. He tiptoed furtively about, asking others to hide their drinking from me for fear that I might be tempted to have one. I appreciated his concern, but finally I explained to him that my sobriety was solid, I was not in danger of picking up a drink, and he need not try to control others' drinking on my account. Prok seemed relieved to hear this, and thereafter shed his protective manner.

At the 1955 AA Twentieth Anniversary Convention in St. Louis, I told my alcoholic story, which was described in detail in *Time* magazine. I was called Earle M., a doctor from California, but Kinsey was an avid reader who regularly enjoyed *Time*. When he read about Dr. Earle M., he knew who they were talking about. The following week I received a letter from him: "Dear Earle: Thank God you finally stopped drinking!" Prok could have said much more but he didn't; he was simply grateful that I was sober.

Prok died the following year.

'Mixing It Up' with AA Members

On one of my many visits to the New York International AA office, Bill W. invited me to join him at an AA men's stag lunch.

A corner of the Brass Rail Restaurant on—I think—Lexington Avenue, was reserved daily at noon for this group of forty to fifty men. The restaurant decor was dark, heavy walnut. The excitement, interest, and sparkling conversation at this luncheon amazed me. There was a feeling of great affection, because all the men were tightly bound together in sobriety. Bill explained that men's stags such as this one (and later, groups for women only) were springing up all over the country. Some men felt uncomfortable talking about male topics and problems in the presence of AA women. Here they were openly discussed. The men laughed at their past antics and, it was obvious to me, felt great relief through sharing in recovery.

Food didn't seem vital to Bill. He drank coffee, he chain-smoked, and he talked *constantly,* almost as though talking to himself. He'd look way off in the distance, or around the room, as if he was addressing a scene that was in his brain. If you asked him a question, he'd frown and look down. He felt no need to look people in the eye. He tended not to address remarks directly *to* people; he looked around instead. Incidentally, his friends knew that you could never safely tell Bill a secret because if you did, your secret would be out. He couldn't keep his mouth shut. But he was more naive than harmful. At times he was like a child, lovable but irritating.

I told Bill that I wanted to start a men's luncheon group in San Francisco. I returned home and proposed this to Jack I., secretary of the San Francisco Central AA Fellowship, who thought it was a good idea. That very day we lunched together at noon in a small downtown San Francisco restaurant, the first meeting of the Friday Men's Luncheon AA Group, which still meets today. Its location has changed several times, as the face of San Francisco has changed. But thirty years later about two dozen men still meet every Friday to enjoy lunch and AA talk.

In Mill Valley we decided to start a men's evening group. The American Legion rented us a room in its hall on Miller Avenue. There, in the late 1950s, the Mill Valley Men's Stag Group of about twenty-five men was formed, and it was an excited, eager bunch. Paper and pencils were provided, and written questions were passed to the chairman, who read aloud each question. No goals and no answers—just a lively group discussion. Questions involved early sobriety as well as problems in emotional recovery, a constant concern. This meeting continued for a good fifteen years until the hall was torn down, the group dispersed, and its members joined other stag groups. I left Mill Valley in the late 1960s, and unfortunately lost track of many original members.

I've always had a lot of fun mixing it up with AA members, especially that Mill Valley Stag Group, and the Children's Hospital Forum, which was organized a bit later. Shortly after I came into AA, the old Tuesday Night Mill Valley Group—my home group—disbanded because the Methodist church sold its building. Paul G. organized the Mud Flats Group (well named!) which met for a while near the northern end of San Francisco Bay, then transferred to the Mill Valley Community Church and became the Monday Night Speaker/Discussion Group.

On weekends many of us met for breakfast in Corte Madera. These unstructured groups were a great place to connect *ad lib*. I carry fond memories of heated discussions with Charlie S., Ewing P., and others. Occasionally we collected at Ewing's home after breakfast, where he would play jazz piano for us, sometimes until late afternoon.

I have a treasured memento of celebrating my first year of sobriety at the Tuesday Night Mill Valley Group. Frank B. and about twenty members of the Seven Seas Club came. Frank and the group gave me an engraved medallion which I carry to this day on my keychain. My initials are on one side. On the other: "Just 24 Hours." No matter where I go, I "carry" Frank, the Seven Seas boys, and the Tuesday Night Mill Valley members with me.

Every Friday night, on lower Golden Gate Avenue in San Francisco, the Central AA office used to host an All Groups Speaker Meeting. Jack I., Central AA secretary, greeted people at the door. About two to five hundred AA members came. This was an excellent chance to meet people from other groups and to renew old acquaintances. Many arrived an hour before the speaker, just to socialize. There was lots of hugging, hand-shaking, laughter, and friendly banter. Inevitably Paul G., who later became Central AA secretary, was there with his friends from Marin County. I always considered that Friday Night All Groups meeting as a sort of party. The speaker was important, but to me, the human interchange was even more so.

How many sober drinkers can count on going to a party that size *every weekend?*

Or, for that matter, to a large weekly Sunday brunch?

The Sunday AA breakfast in Marin County began with a handful of members at the San Rafael King Cotton Drive-In. Within a year it had moved three times and eventually ended up at Howard Johnson's on Highway 101. (Howard Johnson's seems to be a favorite gathering place for AA's all over the country.) A good two hundred people attended. I seldom missed this lively meeting. Several other Sunday morning breakfasts were established there, all with remarkable turnouts. AA grew so fast in Marin County that groups almost stumbled over each other. What a break for the newcomer! *And* for the old-timer!

Giving and receiving tenderness

▲ ▲ ▲ ▲ ▲ ▲ ▲ ▲ ▲

Some of us have great difficulty giving and receiving tenderness. We were taught to be aloof from others; that getting too close to others may endanger us; that we risk being abandoned. Children may grow into adults encased in a wall of pretense that is made of fear, disappointment, and a variety of shoulds, must's, have-to's, and ought-to's.

If we are alcoholics, we discover one day that the wall of pretense, the fears and loneliness, can be dissolved in alcohol. In our cups, we feel at one with the world, able to share love with others. Later the pleasing anesthetic effects of the alcohol wear off, and the wall of pretense returns, but even taller and stronger now.

Eventually, because of the alcoholic's genetic makeup, the symptoms of excess drinking become so excruciating that only more alcohol will dissolve the pain. We become victimized by our drinking rather than relieved by it. Our loneliness increases. We deteriorate physically. We develop severe emotional symptoms directly related to excess drinking—feelings of resentment, self-pity, hatred for others, lack of self-worth. In this condition, some of us—the fortunate ones—seek help from Alcoholics Anonymous.

Believing that it is impossible to give and to receive tenderness, we may at first find that talking about our feelings at AA meetings is enormously difficult and painful. Yet we hang around because we've heard that AA works, and we learn that sharing is our only recourse. When we *do* share with other recovering alcoholics, our walls of fear and pretense begin to crumble. We begin to recover from loneliness. As trust slowly replaces despair, our capacity to give and receive tenderness begins—finally—to grow.

Happy Birthday, Bill W.

"Dear Friends: In this twenty-eighth year of AA, Lois joins with me in thanks to you for sharing this anniversary with us. May we here voice our eternal gratitude that God has been so good! In affection Bill."

Annual AA Dinner program, October 6, 1962, New York City

On October 6, 1962, I spoke at Bill's Annual Dinner, celebrating his twenty-eighth AA anniversary, in the Grand Ballroom of the old Hotel Commodore in New York City. The menu began—and ended—with coffee. A huge pot was on every table throughout the sumptuous five-course meal. I still have the dinner program, signed by Bill, Ebby T., Sam Shoemaker, and Henrietta Seiberling.

Bill had written me on September 24th: "We are so delighted that we are going to see you at the New York Dinner. Can't you drive to Bedford Hills [his home] after the Dinner, or else visit us the next day, Sunday? We sure hope your arrangements will permit a good visit—it's been all too long. Ever yours, [signed] Bill."

Bill and Lois had also invited another dinner speaker, the Rev. Sam Shoemaker, to Bedford Hills. Unfortunately, neither of us made it. Later that evening, after the dinner, Sam went into an oxygen deficit stemming from severe emphysema. They called me, and although his illness was out of my medical sphere, I phoned a local hospital and managed to have him admitted. I was with Sam all night long at the hospital, where he received nasal oxygen and excellent nursing care, and recovered.

Sam and I became very close friends. We exchanged many letters, but I especially treasure the first, written two days after our night in that New York hospital: "I don't know when in my whole life I've come to know anybody so well when I've had so few words with him. Of course your talk drew me like a magnet because of the depth in it and the pulsating, sound understanding of human life and identification with it. This is a great gift of the Spirit and rare, as I needn't tell you."

About a year after that dinner, Sam Shoemaker succumbed to emphysema. His death was an enormous loss to AA.

CARRYING THE AA MESSAGE

"Our Twelfth Step—carrying the message—is the basic service that the AA Fellowship gives; this is our principal aim and the main reason for our existence. Therefore, AA is more than a set of principles; it is a society of alcoholics in action. We must carry the message, else we ourselves can wither and those who haven't been given the truth may die."

Bill W., *The AA Service Manual*, 1969

For years I've done, and still do, a kind of Twelfth Stepping with the *AA Grapevine*. I'll take an issue into a restaurant or store and leave it on my table or on a counter. Then I'll stand nearby to see what happens. People almost always pick it up and read it. Sometimes they call a friend over—another waitress, a salesgirl, or a fellow customer—and read it together. Finally one puts it in her pocket. That's my way of doing mysterious Twelfth Step work. It's fun! I also like to give a copy of the *Grapevine* to new members at an AA meeting, explaining that it's an AA magazine which might be useful for their sobriety. I've sent subscriptions to at least 150 people during my years in AA; I think of that, too, as Twelfth Step work.

In the late 1950s, Jack I. telephoned to say that a local physician, Gil A., was asking for help with his drinking problem. I took Gil to a meeting. He was quiet and a little tremulous, but I could see that he was a seething cauldron within. He maintained a rather glum sobriety in AA for six months. One day he disappeared, then reappeared several weeks later, looking bedraggled. He had drunk his way to Canada, his birthplace, and then returned to continue his binge in Reno. (Eventually he came back to San Francisco. With some reluctance, he rejoined AA and became a devoted member.)

Two weeks later, I told Gil that I was off to Phoenix, Arizona, to be a presenter at the Annual Southwest Obstetrical and Gynecological Conference. I gave him the name and phone number of the hotel where I would be for a week. No sooner had I arrived than Gil phoned my room. He murmured that he was apprehensive and nervous and had decided to come to Phoenix.

We attended the scientific sessions together and I gave two papers.

After the second one, a medical corps naval commander approached us. He was in full dress uniform: gold braid, medals, the works. He said he was a member of "a group" back in San Francisco, and that his "group" might like to hear what I had to say. I asked him the name of the group. He said, rather hesitantly, "It's known as Alcoholics Anonymous." Apparently some things in my talk were AA-oriented!

Gil and I looked at each other. I sidled up to the commander and whispered in his ear, "Are you a drunk?"

Startled, he said that he was.

Gil and I then got a little closer. "We're drunks too, and members of AA," we whispered.

I thought Pat G., M.D., the commander—like Gil and me, he was a gynecologist—would drop through the floor. We three hugged one another and stayed very close for the rest of the conference.

We even attended some AA meetings together in Phoenix.

Back in the San Francisco area, Gil and Pat became very close friends and went to many AA meetings together. Pat left for southern California a few months after we'd met him. Today Gil is a staunch AA member in San Francisco, revered by everyone who knows him. We three remain good friends to this day.

In the mid-1960s, Bill W. telephoned me one day from New York. He'd just made a Twelfth Step call (even Bill made them!) on an airline pilot named Chuck G. (not my old friend Chuck C.)

who was moving to San Francisco. Bill asked if I would take Chuck G. under my wing.

Never have I seen such a bedraggled, wan, depressed person. I found Chuck an apartment in the San Francisco building where I lived part-time, and we became close friends. Chuck had been divorced from a television actress. He watched her daily program, just for a glimpse of this former wife to whom he was still emotionally attached. Eventually he detached from her, stopped watching her show, and became more cheerful. He became a very lively and "going" member of AA.

Meanwhile I'd met Ted F. from Seattle, who had moved to San Mateo, California. Along with Chuck G. and me, Ted, too, was having marriage problems. We shared our troubles and became close friends in the process. Though we three have all left the San Francisco Bay Area, we still remain in contact.

Playing God

▲ ▲ ▲ ▲ ▲ ▲ ▲ ▲ ▲

Like many family members and re-covering alcoholics, I frequently feel I should be responsible for others' emotional well-being. I feel I should rearrange life for them so they can avoid all horror, misery, and pain. Only comfort and hap-piness should be allowed. This, of course, means playing God. In AA, we learn (slowly!) to stop playing that role.

In the Program, I do have one responsibility: extending my hand to another alcoholic and sharing myself with him or her. In the pro-cess, the other person may hear something that will alter his or her life. However, there is no point at all in *demanding* that an alcoholic hear something useful—or even expecting it (the old horse-to-water adage).

During my AA life, I've talked to people who claim I've said something at an AA meeting which changed their lives. When I ask what I said, they invariably quote something I'm quite certain I never did say. Instead, something they *thought* I'd said gave their lives a new direction.

Sharing my life both inside and outside AA helps *me*, strength-ens *my* life, and makes *my* sobriety more valuable to *me*. If the other person grasps something from what I say and uses it, that's heart-ening. But I am not responsible for what my listeners hear. All I can do is to *try* to carry the message to alcoholics, and, as the Twelfth Step says, to practice AA principles in all my affairs.

THE MEANING OF HUMILITY

"We are sure that humility, expressed by anonymity, is the greatest safeguard that Alcoholics Anonymous can ever have."

Twelve Steps and Twelve Traditions, 1953

"Another thing with which most of us are not too blessed is the feeling of humility. I don't mean the fake humility of Dickens's Uriah Heep. I don't mean the doormat variety; we are not called upon to be shoved around and stepped on by anyone; we have a right to stand up for our rights. I'm talking about the attitude of each and every one of us toward our Heavenly Father. . . ."

From a talk by AA co-founder **Dr. Bob S.**, Detroit, 1948,
in *The Co-Founders of Alcoholics Anonymous*,
Originally printed in *AA Grapevine*, June 1973

I couldn't understand myself at times. I seemed restless and irritable. I did rather ridiculous things—nothing vital, but things that demonstrated lack of mature judgment.

For example, as an indication of humility, I decided to refuse positions of honor that were offered to me. Of course this was ridiculous, but that's how I felt. I had accepted the chairmanship of the obstetrical and gynecological department at a local San Francisco hospital. I felt that a "humble" person would not have accepted the position. So I asked the chief of staff if I could resign, and explained why I wanted to do so. He, being wiser than I, convinced me that I was the appropriate person for the job and should not resign. He laughed, took me by the hand, and said, "If you want humility and wish to be humble, you accept that chairmanship and do a good job. That's true humility."

Of course, he was correct, although I didn't know it at the time. However, I did take his advice, plunged into my chairman duties with vigor, and performed well. Whether or not I was cloaked in humility, I am uncertain, but both the chief of staff and I were satisfied.

Another incident occurred with the American Association of Marriage and Family Counselors. I'd been elected national vice-president in 1952-1953, when I was still drinking. I was again elected in 1967-1968. I accepted, but with some reluctance. At the end of the year, the board of directors asked me to run for president of the association. I refused with force, because I believed that a clear, blunt refusal would indicate humility. What a ridiculous decision! Had I accepted, perhaps I could have accomplished some good. By refusing to run, I forfeited that chance.

I realized later that I attain humility only when I listen to everybody and to everything with my ego out of the way. I try to listen in an attempt to learn and expand my knowledge—not to compete, defend, or justify myself.

But at the time my mind was at odds with itself. During the first ten years of my sobriety, in fact, I made several errors of this sort. None were vital or life-taking, but all were based on lopsided deductions. I don't regret my decisions today, because I always learned something from my mistakes and errors in judgment.

I also felt an upheaval within me. I noticed growing disenchantment with organized religions and with absolutes of any kind, including those in AA. I felt odd, lonely, withdrawn. I didn't know it, but I was beginning a long—though sober—struggle.

I was destined to go through a period of irritability in my AA life which, though painful, was productive. For better or for worse, I challenged many basic AA principles. Through these challenges, I learned new ways to interpret and to design my AA Program in a manner unique to me and to my needs.

IRRITABILITY IN AA

THE IRRITABLE PERIOD

In my experience, periods of irritability are sprinkled here and there throughout sobriety, especially during the first few years of recovery. Our protracted emotional withdrawal symptoms may persist, partly because of the malnutrition and varying degrees of anemia associated with drinking alcoholics' poor general health.

The toxicity resulting from temporary physical defects helps to produce many ups and downs in our infatuation with AA and, indeed, with life itself. This adds to a sense of irritability. As our health improves, these symptoms tend to slowly disappear.

A sense of boredom may take over after a few months of sobriety because the AA member wants to speed up recovery. But recovery usually takes its own sweet time and will not be hurried—mine did, anyway!

Irritability is usually accompanied by egocentric demands and is associated with disagreements with fellow AA members or with the AA Program itself. Many AA members feel the urge to drink or to use drugs. How many? According to AA surveys, which are of course anonymous, 45 percent of all new AA members are sober at the end of a year. This means that 55 percent are *not* sober at that time—not great, but the best we have. More encouragingly, approximately 75 percent of all who try the AA Program eventually stay sober.

During the first year or two, everything may seem in disorder at times. We yearn for the return of the romantic interval of AA Infatuation, which seems suddenly to have vanished.

As in a growing child, recovery from alcoholism includes periods of competitiveness—a demand that our "rights" become recognized. Adult temper tantrums can mar our infatuation with AA. Self-esteem may fall to a low level, producing the urge to vie for importance at AA meetings. Our attitude during this time tends to be: I am right. Some of us even exaggerate and distort our drinking/using stories in an attempt to gain recognition.

This period has its growing pains, and growing pains can create a desire to disagree with other AA members, and to demand that other people learn to practice the program in a "correct" fashion (*our* way!). We may challenge the content of certain AA meetings, or we may remain distant from the whole recovery process. Our sharing may be minimal, and our feelings may be concealed.

On the other hand, we can have many happy intervals during which we recognize that sobriety has become a lovely part of our lives. Physical well-being has usually returned. Our insomnia, typical of early sobriety, is generally replaced by nights of restful sleep. A sort of irritable gladness can fill us as we trudge the early paths of recovery. Life in general seems to be improving. New AA friends fill our lives, and AA meetings become pleasant episodes of sharing and learning and loving.

Although attending more AA meetings and sharing how we feel brings comfort during irritable intervals, in my opinion this may be counterbalanced by feeling that AA is taking too much of our time and consequently has become a bore. Usually, however, sharing with others helps us to cope with this bored feeling. After all, troubles shared are troubles halved.

I have experienced all facets of the Irritable interval (still do, at times). The following recounts some of my personal ordeals.

I Could Not Be a Follower

"The point is, there is no prescribed AA 'right' way or 'wrong' way. Each of us uses what is best for himself or herself—without closing the door on other kinds of help we may find valuable at another time. And each of us tries to respect others' rights to do things differently."

Living Sober

Despite troubles and resentments, intervals of deep doubt and despair, and periods of irritability, my basic infatuation with the AA Program has never left me. Nor have I picked up a drink.

In my early Infatuation stage, I listened to and followed the AA "traditionalists" like a child. Their way of living saved my life. Had I not followed their directions for those first three or four years, my life would have become a progressive disaster.

However, around the sixth or seventh year of my sobriety (in about 1960) I began to feel general irritability. I had been a religious zealot in my early AA years. But in time, the inherent religious aspects of AA, which owed their origin to the Oxford Movement, for me began to pall. My unrest was partially directed toward the implied religious aspects of the Twelve Steps, but more particularly toward the traditional "religious die-hards" of AA. Those I met seemed eager to tell everyone how to interpret and to live the AA program. To me, their religious precepts seemed demanding and restrictive.

Close AA friends tried to warn me. I knew that I was stepping on some AA traditionalists' toes. Nevertheless, I began to believe—for better or for worse—that I must develop *my own* AA life, that *I could not be a follower*, particularly of those traditionalists.

This decision caused me turmoil and pain. I had always been afraid to step into the darkness of the unknown and develop my own path; an inner voice told me that I should emulate those who were older and wiser than I. But I felt terribly constrained. I'd had difficulty throughout my life with this concept. At the same time, I wanted to copy and follow some of the AA "spiritual greats," even though this path seemed wrong for me.

I discovered that I must rely solely on my own resources and my own interpretation of life, both in and out of the AA Program. As years went by, I developed *my own brand of AA.* To me, there are as many ways to work the AA Program as there are members of AA. I believe that each member can find his or her own brand, which may differ to some degree from that of other AA members.

My view on this is hardly unique. AA published a pamphlet called *A Member's Eye View of Alcoholics Anonymous* which was "designed to explain to people in the helping professions how AA works." Although the comments are by only one member, "the pamphlet does reflect Fellowship thinking since it has been approved by the AA General Service Conference." For example:

> *"There is no official interpretation which I can blankly pass along to you. There is no party line, no official body of dogma or doctrine to which the members subscribe. No creed that we recite. Even if the surviving co-founder{s} of AA were standing before you tonight, {they} could tell you only how it appears to {them}. I personally consider this absence of orthodoxy one of AA's strongest and most therapeutic principals."*

I felt a growing discomfort with the words "Higher Power." They seemed to work well for others, but gave me a deep sense of separation between me and my God. I am *here* and a Higher Power is something *out there.* My concept of God had become a Healing Power, present in all beings: the ready capacity to repair and to heal. I came to believe that this Divine principle exists everywhere and in everything. For me, then, it was but a short and simple step to recognize God, or Divinity, or Higher Power, *in everything*—animate and inanimate. I am more comfortable feeling connected with everything, being a part of it all.

"Each member uses the Steps in an individual way. The Steps are suggested as a program of recovery. Although experience shows that many AA members' comfort in sobriety depends, to an extent, on their understanding and acceptance of the Steps, no AA member is forced to accept—or even read—them. It is up to the individual to decide when and how the Steps will be used." (from AA's *Is There an Alcoholic in Your Life?*, 1976).

I also experienced difficulty with certain words in Steps Four, Five, Six, Seven, and Eleven. Perhaps my objections to these words could have been called picky, but nevertheless, in those days, I picked and picked away at them.

I felt uneasy about words such as "moral," exact nature of our "wrongs," "shortcomings," and "defects of character." To me, they seemed punitive, inaccurate, and perjorative. If nothing else, they gave me feelings of shame and a sense of innate imperfection.

For example, in the Fourth Step (*"Made a searching and fearless moral inventory of ourselves"*) the word "moral" made me cringe. I had been taught that "moral" meant either "right" or "wrong." I believed that these words could be valuable in the *material* world, but in my *emotional* (and spiritual) world, I could see no right or wrong, irrespective of how I thought or felt.

In the Fifth Step (*"Admitted to God, to ourselves, and to another human being the exact nature of our wrongs"*) I had difficulty with the word "wrongs". I could not see that an alcoholic had done anything wrong unless he had inflicted personal injury on someone. If so, then that—to me—would be wrong. But I failed to see how an emotion could be *wrong*. Or, for that matter, *right*. It just *was* !

I couldn't swallow the idea that any of us have the "defects of character" in the Sixth Step (*"Were entirely ready to have God remove all these defects of character"*). Oh yes, I could readily see that all of us were at different stages of *learning* about life. But to me, these are not defects of character. They are simply stages of learning. Quite a difference, really!

In Step Seven (*"Humbly asked Him to remove our shortcomings"*) it was difficult for me to believe that human beings had "shortcomings." I could see that we were all at different stages of development and awareness. After all, we were expanding all the time. But to me, it was not a shortcoming to be at one place or another. I felt that we all needed to accept where we were at any given instant in our lives, not to label where we were as a short-coming.

And yet, despite my criticisms of the Fourth, Fifth, Sixth and Seventh Steps, I believed that they were valuable. I took the Fourth and Fifth Steps with Bill W., even though I didn't have much to do. I'd come from the Sullivanian school of psychiatry, where you're open with everybody, and also I'd been making amends for years. I didn't believe then and still don't today that I had lots of lurking spirits deep down inside me, bugging me. I *did* have a few little things that I talked to Bill about, and others that I discussed with Chuck C. in California.

For me, Step Eleven (*"Sought through prayer and meditation to improve our conscious contact with God as we understood Him, praying only for knowledge of His will for us and the power to carry that out"*) was concerned solely with religious principles. I found prayer (if used as a petition) and meditation (if used to quiet the mind) of limited value. So I redefined prayer and meditation for myself:

To me, prayer and meditation were identical; each represented a total awareness of everything that happened around and within me. The mind might be quiet or it might not. In either case, total awareness of the current moment brought me indescribable vital-ity, energy, and inspired activity.

On the other hand, I subscribed to the idea that to deny a mystical and magical element in life, its nature totally unknown, was to deny the obvious. After all, what made my heart beat? How did my digestion come about? What mystical element even created digestion and made it function? Digestion and heartbeats are simply present. They are inevitable, and inevitability is part of all of us, I deduced. Together we are a single unit, composed of an infinite number of parts, collectively called human beings. I found it unnecessary to meditate or pray for God's will. If there was such a thing as "God's will," it was and always had been mine to use and to nourish, no matter what the circumstances, drunk or sober! For I was as much a part of it as it was a part of me.

I had always been warned not to "rewrite the Big Book" of Alcoholics Anonymous. But it seems to me that everyone "rewrites" the Big Book to some extent. After all, even though we all read the same words, each of us in our own minds interprets those words to suit our own needs and tastes.

"AA is not a religious society, since it requires no definite religious belief as a condition of membership . . . Included in its membership are Catholics, Protestants, Jews, members of other major religious bodies, agnostics, and atheists.

"The AA program of recovery from alcoholism is undeniably based on acceptance of certain spiritual values. The individual is free to interpret these values as he or she thinks best, or not to think about them at all"

(from *"44 Questions,"*
Alcoholics Anonymous World Services, 1952, revised 1978).

A good number of years elapsed before I could bring myself to reveal my inner doubts about the religious aspects of AA. I felt like a traitor, so I kept most of these objections to myself.

However, slowly, cautiously, and bit by bit, I shared my belief that God, to me, was the essence of being "at one" with everything.

I was very surprised to find that no one seemed to care much!

If any AA member disagreed with or criticized me, he did not do so to my face. But I trembled inside anyway, because I believed that I was breaking away from the mainstream of AA in order to walk my own path. And I was. But I was uncertain that I had the right to do so. I suspect that we all experience similar turmoils and troubles in AA. Today, when I hear younger AA members say how "high" they feel, or, indeed, how depressed they feel, I tell myself, "There go I." Sometimes I tell my own story to these members.

I began to wonder if all of us in AA experience painful emotions until they have run their course. Hadn't we done so with drinking and drugs? Happily, my irritability about the AA Steps mellowed out later in my sobriety, and eventually became unimportant. Later still, after many years in Asia investigating Asian religions, I began to wonder if the ancient Eastern philosophers weren't correct: perhaps abrupt changes are simply the way each of us becomes new, and changes come about through deep, painful, inner turmoil.

I believe that everyone learns from pain. I certainly have. Emotional pain has forced me to accept life as it *is:* on its terms, not on mine.

'A desire to stop drinking'

▲ ▲ ▲ ▲ ▲ ▲ ▲ ▲ ▲

"The only requirement for membership is a desire to stop drinking."

AA Preamble

Early in my AA life, a few "low bottom snobs" (people who drank until they lost nearly everything before getting sober) seemed to sneer at me because my physical trouble with alcohol had not been equivalent to theirs. I found them a menace, for I believed that they implied I did not qualify for AA.

My old friend Mill Valley George was a classic example of how dangerous a limited view of alcoholism signs and symptoms can be. George was constantly criticized by a few people in AA because he simply could not stay sober. He returned repeatedly to the Program, but he never stayed sober longer than five or six months. Although they may have hoped to help George, in my opinion their attitude was not constructive. Their comments depressed George, who eventually died from alcoholism. He had been helpful to others in several ways:

▲ he had had a "desire to stop drinking";

▲ he had kept coming back;

▲ his death tragically illustrated just how powerful alcohol can be for an alcoholic.

DISCONTENT, DEPRESSION, AND ACCEPTANCE

"The deception of others is nearly always rooted in the deception of ourselves."

"The A.A. Way of Life,"
originally published in the August 1961 *AA Grapevine*

I frequently disagreed with my AA friends, often confronted them, and sometimes engaged in verbal battles with them. I seethed inwardly when I heard some "religious" members talk. I wondered if I was being egocentric, presumptive, and absurd. I believed that *I* knew how to deal with people, and I felt that people *needed* me. I thought, *I* can fix you if you'd only listen to *me*. I was hurt when they did not. Bit by bit, I became nervous, irritable, tense, and dissatisfied with life itself. I sensed that there was something amiss in my AA functioning and in my own AA Program. Some members accused me of being on a "dry drunk."* Maybe I was.

Whatever it was, I felt pushed and pulled at the same time.

I also began to feel the strain of my own demands on myself to constantly be "up," "glad," and "emotionally high," as if I had to feel that way in order to maintain sobriety. Pushing myself all the time to be elated was nothing new. All my life I'd tried to appear glad, whether drunk or sober. I'd lived in a state of high rush for too many years, and it was finally becoming too much.

I felt displeased and dissatisfied a good deal of the time.

---

*A dry drunk is a period of irritability, depression or aggressiveness in an alcoholic during a period of abstinence, supposedly accompanied by some signs resembling alcohol intoxication [and/or withdrawal]. *Dictionary of Words about Alcohol.*

However, I never felt the urge to return to drinking.

Despite my discomfort with certain words in some of the AA Steps, and my feeling of being separate from others, I did not dare say so at AA meetings. At that time, disapproval from others was intolerable to me. I was deathly afraid of being reprimanded or shunned.

One day, seeking relief from my burning inner discontent, I read the book *The Power of Positive Thinking* by Norman Vincent Peale, which at that time (1952) had been recently published. I decided that if I could just "think positively," I would find comfort and inner peace, even though I harbored many negative thoughts. For a year or more, I not only preached positive thinking, but I also forced myself to practice it. I smiled almost constantly. I pushed my irritability underground. How did I *really* feel? Worse! The power of positive thinking may be valuable to many, but it was not to me.

Then, one happy day at an AA meeting, I described my attempts to force positive thinking on myself. I explained how awful I felt. "For a long time," I said bitterly, "I've planned to retaliate, to write a book entitled *The Power of Negative Thinking.*" Many in the group smiled and nodded agreement. At long last, I'd broken the ice, and I felt better.

For months thereafter, I discretely divulged portions of my inner pain. No one was surprised. As one AA member told me, "I knew you were feeling uncomfortable all the time. You were on such a false emotional high, I couldn't believe you. Thank goodness you've come back down to us common folk."

And, to a great degree, I had. But there was more to learn: I had to learn to accept myself *exactly* as I was—no more, no less. For me, that was a big job.

I would not erase one moment of the irritable periods in my sobriety. The pain and misery of depression taught me to accept the ups and downs of living moment to moment. Such discomforts were worth their weight in gold.

'Kittos, AA! Thanks, AA!'

Although I was ensconced in my irritable stage, my AA experiences in Europe provided temporary relief. I went to Europe in 1965 for three reasons: to attend my daughter Jane's opera debut in Spoleto, Italy; to present a scientific paper in Helsinki; and to visit AA.

I went to AA meetings in Finland, England, Denmark, France, and Italy. Because AA was much younger in Europe than in the United States, there was a freshness about every meeting. AA's members were like children with new toys, and their enthusiasm was infectious. I found the differences between European and American meetings interesting and exciting. Most European meetings closed with the Serenity Prayer rather than the Lord's Prayer. Of course, either prayer brings AA members very close, especially if members join hands in a large circle. But hand-holding was less common in Europe. To my delight, some European meetings closed with a three- or four-minute silence, reminiscent of encounter and sensitivity awareness groups in the States. What a great idea, I thought.

I went to Helsinki to present a paper at a meeting of the International College of Surgeons. While in Finland I had a remarkable AA experience! In the early 1960s, AA in Finland resembled early AA in the United States: everyone was on fire about the Program and their new-found sobriety.

My heart was so filled that shortly after my European trip, I wrote the following account, "To Finland, With Love," which was published in the December 1965 *AA Grapevine*. Following is an edited version:

"At the Helsinki airport, I was met by an eager AA welcoming group . . . Veikko, known as Kolumbus [after Christopher Columbus—for having 'discovered' AA for Finland in the late 1940s], and a cherubic little man named Aarne (affectionately called Tatta, meaning Grandpa). Kolumbus spoke English very well, but Tatta, the interpreter for the group, spoke English fluently . . . So that I would be able to identify the group, Tatta held a Finnish AA magazine (it looks just like the American *Grapevine*) high over his head. He waved it furiously. Back and forth. Tatta's antics were wonderful, but really unnecessary. I would have recognized that group anywhere. The wide eyes, smiling faces. . . . In an instant I felt at home.

". . . in downtown Helsinki an AA meeting was in progress . . . the group was waiting for me . . . hordes had gathered [four to five hundred people] in fervent anticipation for news of distant AA—especially from America . . . [it was to be] one of the longest and most enjoyable AA meetings that I have ever attended . . . from 7 P.M. to midnight!

". . . The chairman introduced me in Finnish. I didn't understand a word, but I got the idea. He eulogized American AA. Smiles of deep appreciation spread from face to face. And then, my translator and I ascended the speaker's platform. A burst of applause shook the walls. It lasted for several minutes.

" 'They are showing their appreciation for American AA. We have been helped so much,' my translator whispered to me.

". . . I gave a short version of the 'Blackboard Talk.' . . . Never in my AA life have I seen such an attentive, eager, perceptive, appreciative, patient, interested audience. Literally, they drank in every word. They were burning to learn something new about AA and alcoholism. . . . I talked for forty minutes . . . there was another coffee break for ten minutes. . . . The group quickly reassembled. Eagerness and interest had not waned a bit, and already the meeting had been in progress for two and a half to three hours! By request, I told my own alcoholic story. Then, through the interpreter, a flood of questions about American AA were submitted to me. The questions were well thought out. They wanted to know everything. I answered as best I could. I could see that this group really cared. They were devoid of prestige demands. Their humility was natural, and a joy to observe. Implicit in the questions was a desire to know more about AA and alcoholism so that they might carry the message, more successfully, to the Finnish drunk.

"The meeting ended at midnight. Gaiety filled the air: embracing, hand shaking, laughter, and an air of happy tension. I talked with members of the audience either by sign language or through the interpreter. We had our difficulties, but we made it. Slowly each one bade me goodnight and left for home. For a few of us, however, the festivities were far from over: Six of us (including Kolumbus and Tatta) piled into an automobile and drove 110 miles into upper Finland. I was about to experience the greatest thrill of my AA life: a Finnish Sauna bath! One AA member owned a mountain home on the edge of a beautiful lake. By 2 A.M. we were there. To my astonishment the sun had not set! For the first time in my life, I saw an unending day. Tatta explained to me that during the winter the night was almost unending. . . .

"I was hustled into a large room in the hunting lodge. A feast had been prepared.

" 'But first,' said the host (interpreted by Tatta) 'a Sauna bath and a swim!'

"This was a new brand of AA! Off went the clothes, and all of us piled into the Sauna bath. The Sauna bath house was built of a special wood. Along one wall were two long wooden benches. One above the other. In a corner was a hot stove. On it was a mound of white-hot bricks. On the floor, beside the stove, sat a large metal bucket, filled with water which floated a white steel ladle. We climbed the tiered steps and sat next to one another. The host poured a scoop of water over the hot bricks.

"Steam rose toward the ceiling, and almost instantly disappeared. The heat climbed to 110° F.

"I was handed a cluster of birch branches tied at the bottom with heavy twine. Like a bouquet of flowers.

" 'What do I do with this?' I asked Tatta.

" 'Beat yourself all over—like this!'

"And, then, he (and the others) mercilessly beat themselves on their arms and legs and body. With each lash of the birch branches their skin took on a pink hue. I watched in dumb amazement. The host smiled and called to me in Finnish. 'They want you to join them,' Tatta interpreted.

"And I did! Soon I was beating myself from top to bottom with the birch branches. It felt good. My skin tingled. My muscles relaxed. I beat some more. They all watched. Then, with gales of laughter and shouts of glee, they joined me. The host poured another scoop of water onto the hot bricks. Up went more steam. It vanished, but the temperature rose higher. Then more birch-branch beating. More water on the bricks. More steam. More heat. Suddenly the beating stopped, and another AA meeting started! For almost an hour we talked AA—English to Finnish, Finnish to English. 'Here,' I thought, 'is a truly happy bunch of drunks!'—in the nude. Temperature 120 degrees F. Perspiration running freely. Skin red from birch-branch beating. For me, a new brand of AA! I loved it! In spite of the birch beating, the heat and the dripping perspiration, a sort of gentleness permeated the air. There was a spiritual texture to all of this.

"Suddenly, the host opened the Sauna bath door and motioned to me. Kolumbus and Tatta grasped my hand and led me, running, to the end of the pier.

" 'Now we swim!' said Kolumbus.

"And with a loud yelp the three of us dove into the cool water. The others followed. I was refreshed beyond description. Happiness was at a high pitch.

" 'Kittos, AA!' (pronounced "Keytos Ah Ah") cried the swimmers. Over and over and over again.

" 'What are they saying, Tatta?' I asked.

"Tatta swam close to me.

" 'Kittos AA means Thanks AA,' he said. 'They are so grateful for what they have. Without AA none of them would be here. Once again they are alive. Life has taken on a new meaning for them.'

"I knew what Tatta meant. Life had taken on a new meaning for me, too! Here in the woods of Finland, the spiritual side of the AA program penetrated my very soul. I made a full step forward in AA.

" *'Kittos AA!'* I yelled.

" *'Kittos AA,'* they answered.

"Then back to the Sauna bath. All of us. More birch-branch beating. More steam. More heat. More AA talk—and another swim.

" *'Kittos AA. Kittos AA.'*

"Back to the Sauna bath. More birch. More AA talk. And the lake again. Back and forth! Back and forth! The glee, the happiness, the ecstacy grew and grew. By 4 A.M. we were tired! Never have I been so delightfully exhausted in my life! Then, wrapped in sheets, the host led us into the banquet room [between the men's and women's saunas]. Mounds of food waited for us. In one corner of the room a large grill had been built into a stone wall. It was hot, and piled on it was a mountain of sausages. Next to the grill was a table with glasses and gallons of cold apple juice. We needed both! We ate sausages, drank apple juice, talked more AA, laughed and felt good. 'Kittos AA' filled the air. And then the banquet: Bread. Cheese. Cookies. Cakes. Coffee. Tea. The supply was endless! 'They want you to feel welcome,' said Kolumbus.

"And they had!

"By 6 A.M. the meeting ended. (It had started in Helsinki twelve hours before.) We were dressed, in the automobile, and on our way back to Helsinki.

"Never in my life have I slept so soundly. *'Kittos AA'* I murmured as I drifted off to sleep.

"The next evening I again met Kolumbus and Tatta and the Sauna bath AA group and we drove to the lake in upper Finland. On the way Tatta explained the Sauna bath to me.

" 'In Finland, the Sauna bath has a sort of religious significance,' he said. 'Many AAs use the Sauna bath as a symbol of the spiritual life. And you know how the drunk desperately needs the spiritual life?'

"I couldn't have agreed more heartily. 'American AA is spiritual,' I thought, 'but not this much.' What is the origin of the Finnish spiritual life? Why is this little country of less than five million so spiritually endowed? It all seemed so natural. 'Why?' I thought. . . . In America, a Sauna bath is a bath. In Finland the Sauna bath is an opportunity to cleanse the body and commune with God before the Sabbath, the day of rest. I have come to believe that the Finn is 'a natural' for the development of a spiritual way of life. For centuries, the Finn has been trained to observe the spiritual life. From early childhood, the Sauna bath serves as the springboard. No wonder that they have gulped AA with such gusto!

"Soon we were at the lake: more Sauna bath, swims, food and AA talk. By now, I was almost a regular Finnish AA member. By one A.M. we were back in Helsinki. And the sun had never set. How welcome I felt!

"On my third day in Finland, Kolumbus took me to the Helsinki AA office. Tatta and the others had already gathered. A lunch had been prepared: bread and meat, coffee, tea, cookies, cake. But, first, Kolumbus took me on a tour of the office. The others, beaming with pride, followed behind.

"I have seen a lot of AA offices. I like them all. But this one was tops . . . in this Finnish office, I was impressed by the neatness and the organization. This office cared! It was dedicated! As Kolumbus escorted me . . . the group behind us was silent, but I could tell that they were bursting with deep Finnish pride. On a little table at the end of the room lay two open books: the Finnish translations of the Big Book and *Twelve Steps and Twelve*

Traditions—for me—autographed by the entire group! I paused at the table. With great ceremony, Kolumbus grasped my hand, and gently and warmly shook it. *'Kittos, Earle,'* he murmured.

"And then he handed me the two books. A gift from the AAs of Finland. This could have been a tear jerker, but a round of applause broke the tension. And then came lunch: one of the most gala affairs that I have ever seen. A gaiety that was spiritual filled the room. Though I could not speak Finnish, I no longer needed a translator. I was one of them and they knew it!

"After lunch the little AA group took me to the airport. Each of them had a small token of remembrance for me. In turn I shook each hand. Then two of them stood forward and in Finnish delivered an eloquent speech of thanks for my visit. Ending with, 'Kittos.' Tatta translated. 'They appreciate your visit, and what you have given them,' Tatta whispered into my ear. I smiled at them. We embraced one another. And with the Finnish Big Book and the Twelve-and-Twelve tucked under my arm I was off.

"On the plane I had a lot to think about. Years ago, in a California city, only a few miles from my home, a man named Usko had written a letter to a hopeless drunk [Kolumbus] in Finland. From that letter, AA had been introduced to the Finns. Seventeen years later I had visited Finland and had received the most tremendous AA lift that I have had in years. Usko's long Twelfth Step call had boomeranged back to me (a fellow Californian) by way of Finland.

" 'But isn't it odd,' I thought, 'they have seen fit to thank me for what I have done for them. They and Usko deserve the thanks.' For a moment I felt guilty, but the guilt vanished as I thought, 'Isn't that the way it is in AA?'

"I savored this thought during my flight. As we passed over the sea leaving Finland in the distance, I looked back toward Helsinki. I couldn't help but murmur to myself:

" *'Kittos, Usko!'*

" *'Kittos, Finland!'*

" 'Kittos, AA!' . . ."

Several years later, Kolumbus came to San Francisco and spoke at our Friday All Groups meeting. I introduced Usko W. as Kolumbus's original sponsor, and told the meeting how Usko had made a remarkable Twelfth Step call on Kolumbus seventeen years before I visited Finland.

Usko took over and described how he had migrated from Finland to San Francisco. There, he'd realized that he was in serious trouble with alcohol. He joined AA, became very active in the Program, and wrote his friend Veikko (later dubbed Kolumbus) in Helsinki. Usko described his trouble with alcohol, which Kolumbus had known about, in a long letter that also told about AA in the United States and how sobriety was maintained by spiritual maneuvers. Kolumbus then realized that he, too, was in serious trouble with alcohol. And that letter from Usko, many thousands of miles away, constituted a Twelfth Step call—a magical landmark in Veikko's life. Kolumbus initially maintained sobriety by simply reading and re-reading Usko's letter.

(When I met him several years later, Veikko showed that tattered, worn letter to me. It was in a frame in the Helsinki Intergroup office.)

Eventually Kolumbus and his friend Tatta, who was also sober, had started an AA meeting in Helsinki. From that meager beginning, Alcoholics Anonymous spread rapidly throughout Finland. Happily so, because the incidence of alcoholism in Finland is very high.

Tatta translated the Big Book (*Alcoholics Anonymous*) into Finnish. I was honored when my story, "Physician, Heal Thyself!" was included in the Finnish edition.

Although Kolumbus could speak English reasonably well, he chose to speak Finnish that night in San Francisco. Usko translated. It was a marvelous meeting. Kolumbus and I corresponded for years after he returned to Finland.

AA in Europe

"AA in France, we hear, had several false starts—mostly among Americans—but refused to die. A sight-seeing member from New York's Greenwich Village reported visiting the famous Harry's Bar in Paris in 1947, where he was shown a giant pitcher used for beer-guzzling bouts. He peered hard to see what was at the bottom of the less-than-clean 'loving cup,' and it turned out to be a brew-soaked copy of the first edition of the Big Book. No one ever explained how it got there, but it was rumored that an earlier tourist had chosen that way to 'resign'. . . ."

"Round and Around We Go," *AA Today*, AA Grapevine, 1960

From Helsinki I went to Copenhagen. AA was very new there. I met with members of a small, devoted group, who spoke English out of deference to me, and I told them about AA in the United States. They hung on every word. They had been in touch with Kolumbus, and were eager to see AA expand in Denmark as it had in Finland.

After only one day and night in Copenhagen, I flew to Paris, where I attended an English-speaking AA meeting. The chairman of the meeting that night was an old friend of mine, Dan, a newspaperman from the San Rafael *Independent Journal* near San Francisco. Neither of us had known that the other would be visiting Paris. Imagine our glee when we spied one another! AA throughout the world brings its members together in strange ways!

I was a speaker that night. The meeting was long, as other AAs—both French and English—also shared their stories. We closed with three minutes of silence, a novel—and nice—experience.

Unexpected encounters are not confined to AA meetings. I was in Paris for three days. On my last day, sauntering down a street near the Paris Opera House enjoying the Paris springtime, I went to an outdoor cafe, ordered a cup of cappuccino, and glanced at two women at a nearby table. To my surprise, they were my wife and my mother! I hurried over to their table. "How do you do, ladies," I said, as casually as I could manage. They both screamed, and a big hugging scene followed (nothing new to Parisians). They were about to leave for Rome, where we had planned to meet, but I still had medical business in Paris, so I said jauntily, "See you in Rome!"

The AA General Service Office in New York had given me a Rome contact: Langston M. He and a writer named Peter D. and I had an "open" AA meeting—just the three of us—in an outdoor cafe under the stars. With enthusiasm, they described AA meetings in Rome as "untraditional but effective." They said that AA's growth was slow, partly because the cultural requirement of wine with meals made abstinence from alcohol difficult for Italians. Nonetheless, the groups were growing, and an AA member was translating the Big Book into Italian.

My wife, my mother, and I toured Rome and then took a train to Spoleto, where my daughter Jane's operatic debut was a great success. Jane sang Desdemona in *Otello* at the Spoleto Festival, conducted by Thomas Shippers of the Metropolitan Opera. (Jane's Spoleto debut was a prelude to her competing in the Moscow Tchaikovsky Festival in 1966, where she won first prize for voice.) After the *Otello* opening, I left my wife and mother to attend the remaining performances and continued on alone to London.

My visit to London and environs was a joy. I stayed at the New Bedford Hotel on Tottenham Court Road, and—as usual—walked a great deal through sections of the city. I felt most comfortable in London. As I turned a corner and looked up a street, I felt certain I'd been there before—as if I was making a return visit to another life. I probably recognized certain streets because I'd seen similar ones so often in magazines and books. But who knows? Maybe I *was* there in a former life, if there is such a thing.

The AA General Service Office in New York had told the London AA office that I'd be coming to England. Two AA members had arranged several talks in London for me, all of which were well received. I also enjoyed some interesting luncheons with London AA members. I noticed two differences between British and American AA: in London, only the text of the Big Book was used—the stories had been eliminated; and at the end of each meeting, the group recited the Serenity Prayer instead of the Lord's Prayer. I told my final London audience that I'd been intrigued by their "foreign" accents. When that brought down the house, I realized to my chagrin that the only one with an accent was me!

I met Max M. Glatt, M.D., a dedicated physician who later created the well-known Glatt Chart of alcohol addiction. The chart shows stages in the progression of drinking as well as of recovery. He was a British pioneer in medical treatment of alcoholics. Max arranged for me to address his patients at several hospitals, talks which were followed by lively discussions at a time when little was known over there about the disease of alcoholism.

While in England, I even saw a ghost! Through AA I met Alec and Ann F. and their daughter Fiona, who invited me to visit their Hampshire home, Orchard Cottage, for a taste of English country life. The British are intrigued by ghosts. The house, in the middle of an old apple orchard, was originally U-shaped, but a bedroom now replaced a very large apple bin in the former U.

Two hundred years before, the orchard and bin had been tended by a local gardener, who felt the area was really *his* home. Occasionally Alec and Ann caught a glimpse of the gardener's friendly spirit turning a corner upstairs, but when they scurried to meet him, his image would evaporate. Though they laughed about it, they told me they were "partially convinced that this gardener-ghost lived in the house."

I slept in the bedroom that had replaced the apple bin. In the middle of my first night, I woke—sensing that someone stood behind me. He was bearded, and his left hand was on my shoulder. He seemed to be asking me to leave, but in a gentle fashion. I have no idea how I saw him or knew that he was bearded, because he was directly behind me.

Next morning, my hosts were not surprised. They said that the caretaker's spirit had visited me. Their belief carried more impact with me when we found a fresh tear in the wallpaper behind my bed!

Did the gardener-ghost live there? I don't know—maybe so!

While in Hampshire, I spoke on alcoholism to inpatients at several hospitals. My hosts treated me like a king.

When I finally left England for San Francisco, my heart was filled with joy and fulfillment from my experiences, especially AA in England and on the continent.

My contact with AA in Europe stimulated my interest in traveling and visiting AA worldwide. My travels had made me aware that AA meetings can vary, and that although there are many brands of Alcoholics Anonymous, a common thread—sobriety through spiritual awareness—is woven into each.

I Didn't Sober Up to Find Peace!

For most of the 1960s, I was so busy and active in all facets of my life that I lived in a kind of cyclone. I apparently seemed reasonably cool and controlled on the surface, but inside I was seething. On one hand were doubts, despairs, and attempts to discover where I fit. On the other was ecstacy in discovering new meanings in AA life. I'm sure that had my AA acquaintances been aware of my inner moods, they would have advised me to settle down and apply the AA principles. Or at least to discuss my problems with an AA friend. But I could not bring myself to do either. I found it necessary to live alone with my problems and pain. I still do, to a great degree. AA recommends discussing painful emotional problems at the time they occur—I find this difficult. Only when inner pain and despair give way to new insights can I discuss the whole picture with someone. I think I go through pain in order to expand my awareness. I can then share my experiences with someone else, who may in turn gain strength and hope from them.

Often I was at cross-purposes with myself. If I found a new way of thinking that promised emotional relief, I would try it on for size. *The Power of Positive Thinking* was one example. Other gimmicks rose out of Eastern and Western philosophies. Or, I might hear a speaker say something that appealed to me at an AA meeting or conference. I'd rush home to imitate him, only to discover that I could not "be" him. Then I'd feel hollow and despairing again.

I seemed to recoil at simply being *myself*. And so it went through much of the 1960s—up and down, in and out, trying anything and everything. Some of my discoveries were partially valuable, some not in the least. This interval of my AA life was a wild, irritable one. I often wondered how those around me stood my antics, since I found it difficult to stand them myself.

In the early 1960s, I wrote an article called "Thank God for Despair," which I planned to send to the *AA Grapevine*. At that time I was afraid to disclose my deep despair to my AA friends. *I* was above such things, I thought, so I hid the article in a desk drawer. I had come to think that a good AA member is *always* happy. What a mistake that was! The article stayed in my desk for some time before I submitted it. Published in the June 1965 *Grapevine*, "Thank God for Despair" has been reprinted in the magazine several times. When I read it over today, more than twenty years later, I wouldn't change anything in it.

Thank God for Despair

"It is amazing and a little depressing to see so many of our members drive themselves like madmen for perfect peace of mind and absolute serenity. Bags under their eyes, frowns on their foreheads—driving, driving. They act as though peace of mind were the answer to life. Where do they get such a ridiculous idea? The Big Book doesn't mention it. Neither does *Twelve Steps and Twelve Traditions*. I can't find it [elsewhere] in our literature, either.

"I haven't the slightest idea what the words 'peace of mind' mean! I haven't the remotest concept of serenity. Contentment is simply another word to me most of the time. Now and again, after a particularly rough emotional interval (and I have them constantly), I repeat the Serenity Prayer or say 'Easy Does It' or 'First Things First' or any of our other slogans, and peace and serenity come over me. I feel glorious and wonderful and calm and loving and giving. I even wonder what I was so upset about. I think that I have at last found the answer to life, and vow to hang on to my ecstasy for the rest of my life. And I mean it!

" 'Now you have it. Hang on to it. You fool, do you mean to tell me that it took you all this time to tumble to the real meaning behind the AA program?' I murmur to myself. And I'll hang on to what I have for about sixty seconds—sometimes longer, maybe a day or even two—but not much longer. Inevitably, the same old drag will come over me, and I'm off to the races on another tangent, fighting, struggling, snarling, and making a mess of things for myself—*inside,* that is. On the *outside,* I'm the epitome of discipline and control.

"At our closed meeting, unsigned questions are submitted and then tossed out to the group by the chairman, for discussion. Any question or any answer is accepted. Sometimes, there is a hassle about the proper answer to a question, but usually no one especially cares if a hodgepodge of answers pile up, and everyone seems to have a pretty good time. For several years, I have saved the questions. The other day, I went over them. I wasn't at all surprised to find that over half of them were queries about peace of mind. For instance, I was talking to one of our old-time members recently. He said that in spite of his years of sobriety, he feels terrible most of the time. He told me that he is continually fighting one thing or the other. He wanted to know if I thought that he would ever find contentment or peace of mind. I told him that I doubted it—maybe snatches of it, but contentment for long periods was probably out.

"We are a bunch of malcontents. The alcoholic is never satisfied for long intervals. Probably no one, alcoholic or not, is satisfied for long intervals. Otherwise, how would we learn and grow? The bottoms that I have hit since coming into AA have been far worse than anything that I dreamed possible when I was drinking. Why? Because when I was drinking, I could always dive into the bottle and forget, but I don't want that anymore. I want to remember! I want to live life to its fullest, and if this means lack of peace of mind, that's all right with me. Never in my blackest moments have I had the slightest desire to drink. I'm too busy fighting and struggling and feeling and seeing to want to erase life with booze.

"An AA member needn't concentrate on finding serenity! What would he do with it if he had it? Probably curl up and die. The drunk is never satisfied. That's the way he grows. He fights and loses and learns, or he fights and wins and learns. But the point is that he loves the fight. He may complain about it, but take it away from him and he's in trouble. He didn't sober up to find peace. He sobered up so that he could live life to the fullest. And this means struggle and unrest and worry and concern, sprinkled here and there with snatches of peace. But these snatches of peace are just rest periods before the next fight begins.

"We love the combat. Our trouble is that we linger under the delusion that we are supposed to be happy. So, when we are unhappy and deluged with troubles, we feel that we are not on the program. Any member who is in a state of constant placidity may be on the program, but I do not believe he is living life to its fullest. He may be sober, but he's static. 'Part of the fun in life is the misery of the battle. If I had my life to live again, I wouldn't change one single second of it. I would live it exactly the same way, because every second that I live has brought me closer and closer to what I have now. I like being a malcontent. I wouldn't give it up for the world. Discontent is my greatest friend. I told this to one of my friends recently, and he said, 'You sound like you are in a constant state of despair.'

"I grabbed him by the coat and said, 'If I am, thank God for despair. I'll take some more of it. Happiness is great, but it's like ice cream—I get tired of it. If the meat and the potatoes of life are despair and if despair has brought me what I have today, I want more of it. I'll give you a scoop of my ice cream if you'll give me a plateful of your meat and potatoes.'

"Live, and you change. But you can't change until you have whole-heartedly accepted yourself exactly as you are. You may not like what you accept. But you must accept it if you want change.

"Now, if I am a guy who is thirsty for life at its fullest, and if I am moving from one level to the next by way of despair, I hereby announce that I will accept all of the despair that you can pile on me. I need it. I yearn for it. I love it. Not because I like feeling tied up in knots, but because I am obsessed with learning and living and feeling and growing, and apparently, discontent and despair and unrest are the very ingredients of the fuel that I need.

"I can understand that a resentment at not having a constant state of serenity might lead to disillusion and then to a drunk, but I wholeheartedly disagree that diving into life and wrestling with it leads to a drunk. Malcontents don't slip; they change! They fight it out, and they love the struggle.

"If, however, they demand that life be easy for them and if they demand that they be spared unrest and discontent and despair, they are in for trouble. God help the sober drunk who thinks that he has it made. God help the sober drunk who thinks that, because he has found the AA program, all clouds will remain pink. I like the color pink myself, but it palls after a while. Give me a good black one. . . .

"The AA program gives us tools to work with, measuring rods to level our lives with. The AA program is basic stuff. We all need basic stuff as a leveler. But if the AA program meant that once we found it, our troubles would be over, what would be the need of our meetings, our Big Book, our Twelve Steps, and our Twelve Traditions? We need those things as levelers because we lose our way easily as we build and grow. And when we build and grow, we despair easily. It's our nature to do so. But to refind the program—to refind the Twelve Steps and the Twelve Traditions, to refind the deep significance of our AA slogans, to refind one another at meetings—means that, having had enough of despair, we have come home once again, in order to prepare ourselves for the next fight. We try. We lose. (Sometimes we win.) But the point is that we try. And in the process, we struggle and despair all over the place. Don't worry about it."

A THIRTY-YEAR MARRIAGE AND DIVORCE

"For some reason, we alcoholics seem to have the gift of picking out the world's finest women. Why they should be subjected to the tortures we inflict on them, I cannot explain."

Bob S., M.D.,
"Dr. Bob's Nightmare" from *Alcoholics Anonymous*

"When I was a child, my parents put on a facade of happiness. Everyone thought they were model parents; everyone was surprised about their break-up. I wasn't."

Jane M., Dr. Earle's daughter

For many reasons, my marriage had long been a strain both for my wife, Mary, and for me. Although we had a deep regard for one another, we found it virtually impossible to communicate on a personal level.

Mary was a very kind, giving person. Before we married in 1940, she had devoted her life to helping her family recover from a horrendous financial shock. Her father died suddenly, the year after the 1929 stock market crash, leaving his wife and three daughters financially handicapped. Mary's wonderful, resilient mother did her best to support the family, but her singular efforts were not enough. Mary came to her mother's aid. Caring for her mother and two younger sisters became paramount in her life, particularly after her sisters were diagnosed as psychotic in the early 1940s. After we married, I helped her; medical bills for my sisters-in-law were horrendously high. But with all of this concern and focus on the extended family, and later on our own daughter, who was born in 1942, little energy or time remained for much of a husband-wife relationship. Throughout our thirty-year marriage, that relationship never really developed. The tragedy of three stillbirths compounded our problems.

Mary once told me: "I have great respect for you as a doctor, but none as a human being."

[First my drinking, then my "sobriety activities"]played a part in keeping my wife and me separated. I threw my enormous energy into activity: my busy obstetrical and gynecological practice, marriage counseling (really!), AA, racing pigeons, local theater, research for Kinsey, daily exercise, travel, some romances, and goodness knows what else. Unfortunately, I had as little room for her in my life as she had for me in hers.

For example, in "Physician, Heal Thyself!"—my story in AA's Big Book—I wrote in 1955:

"Shortly after I was starting to work on the program I realized that I was not a good father; I wasn't a good husband, but, oh, I was a good provider. I never robbed my family of anything. I gave them everything, except the greatest thing in the world, and that is peace of mind. So I went to my wife and asked her, wasn't there something that she and I could do to somehow get together, and she turned on her heel and looked me squarely in the eye, and said, 'You don't care anything about my problem,' and I could have smacked her, but I said to myself, 'Grab on to your serenity!' She left, and I sat down and crossed my hands, and looked up and said, 'For God's sake, help me.' And then a silly, simple thought came to me. I didn't know anything about being a father; I don't know how to come home and work week-ends like other husbands; I don't know how to entertain my family. But I remembered that every night after dinner my wife would get up and do the dishes. Well, I could do the dishes. So I went to her and said, 'There's only one thing I want in my whole life, and I don't want any commendation; I don't want any credit; I don't want anything from you or Janey for the rest of your life except

one thing; and that is, the opportunity to do anything you want always.' And now I am doing the darn dishes every night! . . ."

For years, I saw psychiatrists and marriage counselors, but to little avail. Mary was not interested in treatment for herself. She went to a marriage counselor once and said she couldn't stand it. There was no Al-Anon in our area until the late 1950s, but even when it was available she had no interest in going.

I became painfully aware, when I was several years sober, that the distance between us was growing. We were mutually disinterested in our marriage, and since we weren't especially comfortable around one another, we tended to travel in different directions. I felt responsible and guilty as I watched our marriage crumble, but I didn't know what more I could do to try to save it.

I had heard as an AA newcomer that male alcoholics tended to relate poorly to women. Consequently, I was celibate for the entire first five years of my sobriety.

In the early 1960s I felt forced, by my own sex urges, to find a lover.

Libby was an actress, and a loving, caring woman. She was largely responsible for bringing me home to myself. Despite my insistence that I remain married, Libby was willing to stay with me, nurture me, and comfort me. She was important to my life and my sobriety. Unlike Mary, Libby went to open AA meetings with me now and again. After her first, she said, "I wish I was an alcoholic in order to enjoy what AA offers."

Unbeknownst to my wife, I set up an apartment in San Francisco. I spent half my time there with Libby, and half in Mill Valley with my family. But after about three years, when I was back on my psychological feet, so to speak, Libby decided to continue her acting career. She had been accepted at RADA—the Royal Academy of Dramatic Arts in London—a marvelous opportunity for her. I spent my annual vacation accompanying her to London. I wanted to help her move in and feel secure there. Together we found Libby an apartment, and we did the rounds of theater: the

Royal Shakespeare at Stratford-on-Avon, the Old Vic, and London's West End contemporary theater. We also went to open AA meetings together.

Finally the time came for me to go home to California. With no fanfare, we went to the airport together, kissed good-bye, and never saw one another again. Years passed before I recovered from that love affair. To this day, I still think of Libby with deep affection. I could not have asked for a more loving companion. Yet at the time, I could not bring myself to divorce my wife. I was locked into that old credo that a good man never gets a divorce. I now believe that Mary and I should have divorced far sooner than we did. Some sober alcoholics can repair the marital damage that results from drinking. This was not true for Mary and me, although we *could* join forces to raise our daughter, Jane, and to help Mary's family.

An AA friend said, "Once I came into AA, I found I didn't have to marry as much." I discovered the reverse: once I came into AA, I found I had to marry a lot!

But in sobriety I found it necesary to re-evaluate my life from many standpoints. One was the state of my thirty-year marriage.

My crippled relationship with Mary was an intense heartache to me, and I feel certain that it was for her too. The saddest event of my life was the termination of that marriage in the late 1960s, during my fifteenth year of sobriety. I felt incomplete and unfinished, and I deeply regretted that Mary and I did not make it together.

Mary died almost twenty years after our divorce. The day of her death, I sat alone at my desk at three o'clock in the morning, sobbing with despair, remorse, and grief. I mourned not only Mary's passing, but also the failure of our marriage. At the same time, I felt a sudden release and I grew quiet inside: I had come to terms with my first marriage. I finally realized clearly that I'd always loved Mary deeply, but that—sadly—we simply could not manage being married to each other.

A daughter's view ▲ ▲ ▲ ▲ ▲ ▲ ▲ ▲ ▲

"Everyone thought we had a perfect storybook family. We didn't, of course.

"The most painful thing to me about their divorce was its timing: 1966, when I won the gold medallion at the International Tchaikovsky Voice Competition in Moscow. Pianist Van Cliburn was the first American to win that competition in 1958, and his career took off in a legendary fashion. I was the second American, and the first vocalist, to win. I, too, was catapulted to stardom. I badly needed the emotional support of my parents, but they had other preoccupations. My mother felt that her elderly mother and sister 'needed' her more than I did. She believed that I could survive without her help, but that they could not. This turned out to be true, and it seems to be the story of my life.

"My father was preoccupied with his own catharsis. Some people have told me it wasn't easy for him to see me become such a success—to be so in the public eye. During the many years I lived in Europe, I saw him twice. My mother never came over, which encouraged my father to feel that he'd been supportive in contrast. I've understood, somehow, but it's been hard.

"I think, too, it should be noted that this is *his* book and he's given *me*, however it comes across, an opportunity to air my feelings.

"I believe he's been searching for something all his life, and I hope he's finally found it. Our paths are still separate, though I don't ever totally close a door because he *is* my father."

Jane M., Dr. Earle's daughter

BEFORE ALCOHOLISM
WAS CONSIDERED A DISEASE

"The aggressions, feeling of guilt, remorse, resentments, withdrawal, etc., which develop in the phases of alcohol addiction are largely consequences of the excessive drinking . . . By and large, these reactions to excessive drinking—which have quite a neurotic appearance—give the impression of an 'alcoholic personality,' although they are secondary behaviors superimposed over a large variety of personality types which have few traits in common . . ."

> E. M. Jellinek, "Phases of Alcohol Addiction,"
> *Quarterly Journal of Studies on Alcohol,* 1952

Beginning early in my sobriety, in the mid-1950s when I met Dr. Robert Gordon Bell from Canada, I became increasingly convinced that alcoholism and all other drug addictions were:

1. physical—predominantly *genetic in origin*;

2. psychological—with *mental and behavioral aberrations resulting from* the constant and excessive intake of alcohol/drugs.

Psychologists of the behavioral school preached the reverse: that deep emotional aberrations were responsible for the development of an addiction. Their point of view made little sense to me, professionally or personally. So I became obsessed with discovering the causation and nature of alcoholism and other addictions, and with wanting to settle the question.

For many years, I pored over scientific books, journals, and articles concerning alcohol/drug addiction. I also read AA literature. One day in about 1957 or '58, I found a statement on page

62 in the Big Book about alcoholism: that selfishness, self-centeredness, fear, self-delusion, self-seeking, and self-pity were "the *root of our troubles.*" I could not believe my eyes! To me, these statements were incorrect. After all, if selfishness, self-centeredness, fear, self-delusion, self-seeking, and self-pity caused alcoholism, then almost *everyone* should develop the disease! Since only 10 to 15 percent of the population were alcoholic, how could all these common emotions quoted in the Big Book be the primary cause of alcoholism? The *causes* must rest elsewhere.

To my horror, I also noted on page 64 in the Big Book that "our liquor was but a *symptom*" of such psychological aberrations. With more and more scientific data on addiction and cross-addiction becoming available, I just couldn't buy that! Based on the most current information of the time, I believed that alcoholism—all addiction, for that matter—*was not a symptom of anything, but was a primary disease in itself.* Our resentments, or selfishness, or self-centeredness, or self-pity were *not* the *cause* of alcoholism. These emotions were *by-products* of excessive, compulsive ingestion of alcohol and/or other drugs.

I began to believe, even then, that addictions of all types are predominantly genetic in origin and familial in nature; that susceptibility to addiction is transferred from one generation to the next. In this respect, alcoholism/drug addiction resemble diabetes—an error in metabolism. Of course, not all members of a family-at-risk develop an addiction, just as not all develop diabetes. In my family's case, for example, although both my parents and many other relatives on both sides of the family were alcoholics, my brother was not an alcoholic. At that time, scientific research that I'd seen showed that about 85 percent of alcoholics could discover alcoholism or some type of chemical addiction in their parents or grandparents (the previous two generations). However, the other 15 percent could not find this connection.

I knew that many alcohol and drug addicts suffered deep guilt about their addiction, and felt responsible for the development of their disease. I became convinced that *because susceptibility to the disease is inherited, alcoholics and drug addicts are not responsible for their alcohol/drug addiction, but they are responsible for their recoveries!*

I carried this genetic message to addicts of all types. Beginning in the late 1960s, I studied scientific findings on the genetic factor in alcoholism, the abnormal metabolism of alcohol, and the deficiencies in the brain's neurotransmitters—especially the endorphins. I had used the phrase "x-factor" in my early Blackboard Talks, which had implied the genetic nature of addiction. Now I updated my Blackboard Talk, believing that alcohol and drug addicts need to know that they are *not* "emotional cripples," and that they have the right to understand the biological etiology of their addictive disease, and consequently to be relieved of any burning guilt. In my opinion, knowledge neutralizes personal guilt.

Many so-called "traditional AA members" said that I should not give my Blackboard Talk at AA meetings. They said that it conflicted with AA Traditions and brought professionalism into the Program. Some even accused me of desecrating the Big Book.

To me, *Alcoholics Anonymous* was, and is, a beautiful tome. I love the book, and knew and loved its author, Bill W. However, it had been written in the late 1930s. By the 1950s and early 1960s, I felt that the Big Book had some inaccuracies about *causation* of alcoholism. It had the cart before the horse, as far as I was concerned. And considering when the book was written, that was understandable. Bill W. founded AA and wrote the Big Book at a time when everyone thought the alcoholic/addict was an "emotional cripple." Today, new information has replaced those old myths, and the emotional cripple concept has been abandoned by most scientists.

For months and months I experienced mixed emotions. I could not bring myself to say that I thought there were errors in the Big Book. In those days I found it difficult to stand by my convictions. But hiding them caused me pain and turmoil, which could have been relieved by courageously stating my position and letting the chips fall where they may. I knew that my convictions were based on some sound scientific evidence, and I should have stated them honestly—but I could not.

Today I don't mind stating my position strongly and clearly. Many still disagree with me, but that's all right. After all, no one *really* knows with certainty which factors cause addictive disease. The final answer is not in—yet.

Today my irritability about those statements in the Big Book has disappeared. Now and again, when I hear an irritable AA member tell me (or someone else) how I *should* interpret and use the Big Book and AA Steps, I yawn! To me, that person is simply living the Program in the only way that fits for *him*. I don't blame him for wanting to alter *my* way of interpreting AA or the Big Book. After all, I've been there myself. But I still yawn! During my Irritability period in AA, I twisted, bent, and stretched the Program. I found it pliable, durable, and embracing in return. It simply would not give. I am glad that I attempted to "break" AA, because in putting it to the test and validating its elasticity, I carved out a way of AA living that has worked beautifully for me.

INVENTIVENESS IN AA

THE INVENTIVE PERIOD

In the Inventive Period, cooperation with others develops and competition wanes. Some of us begin to associate with AA members of like mind, to establish new sorts of AA groups, and to consider that the Big Book, *Alcoholics Anonymous,* should be altered, if not literally rewritten. Indeed, during this phase, some AA members may challenge the entire framework of AA and want to change it. Those who start new groups the way I did may be attempting to do so.

The Inventive Period can be filled with varying moods: a sense of exhilaration, adventure, resentment, and hurry. The hyperactivity evident in the Infatuation and Irritability periods may be increased in the Inventive period, so that some of us exist in a state of frenzy that we feel we cannot stop.

In spite of being tight and tense, the Inventive Period offers many happy moments. We may combine our efforts with other irritable, inventive members, establish new groups, and even feel that former AA friends will abandon us. But if so, our new irritable and inventive friends will fill that gap.

At times we may feel disenfranchised and separate, from ourselves and from others. During this phase, some AA members give in and decide to become followers. I disliked becoming stuck in one place, for I believed that I was growing very little, and remaining rigid and traditional. Thus I decided to kick over the traces. Activity and creativity saw me through painful learning periods. Some AA members call the Inventive Period a "dry drunk." Perhaps so for some, but for me, I doubt it.

My Irritable and Inventive Periods dovetailed and represented a continuum in many respects.

The Inventive Period in my Alcoholics Anonymous development was filled with rush, resentment, exhilaration, and chance-taking. The high activity level which characterized my Irritable period increased with the Inventive interval. I was harried, hurried, distracted—but I was not to be stopped! The interval led me to new insights. Here are some examples of what happened in my own Inventive period.

JOYOUS AND TUMULTUOUS SOBRIETY

"To every member of AA, there comes a day—admitted by some, kept secret by others—when he begins to ask himself a gnawing, troubled question. Sometimes, the words are: 'Is AA enough?' Other times, the question takes a more fatalistic overtone: 'Is AA all there is going to be?' And in still other instances, it comes out simply as 'What now, little man, what now?' "

A Member's Eye View of Alcoholics Anonymous

In the last half of the 1960s, after about fifteen years of joyous though rather tumultuous sobriety, I found myself wound up tight as a spring. My normally high energy level tripled. Perhaps I was in an agitated middle-aged crisis. Some would certainly say so.

During mid-sobriety in AA (somewhere between ten and twenty years) we may suffer extremes. We might feel fresh, new, excited, joyous, and look forward to change. Or—because of pain—we might give in, collapsc, fail to grow, and become static, doggedly conservative, and traditional.

In the mid-1960s I began to share very openly my dislike for the so-called religious aspects inherent in the Twelve Steps. I had felt this way in the early 1960s, during my Irritable period; now I spoke up about my personal discomfort with the words "Higher Power." However, I recognized, and said so at meetings, that most AA members love the very words which caused me such discomfort. I explained that in my early years of sobriety, I had been religious because I thought this was required in AA. Although deep down I had had serious personal misgivings, I could not bring myself to say so at meetings at the time. But now, in mid-sobriety, I spoke out freely. In fact, I was rather bullish and curt. I argued, engaged in verbal battles, and carried resentments toward those whom I felt were too traditional. Consequently many old friends abandoned me, but I made new friends who had experienced similar irritable doubts. I felt extremely lonely at times—disenfranchised and separate from myself and from others. However, my sobriety was solid. Never since June 15, 1953—the last day of my drinking—has the urge to drink alcohol returned.

I attended many AA meetings throughout this Irritable/Inventive period. They helped, to some degree. But my anger and resentment made me feel *apart from* everything, rather than *a part of* something.

During the first fifteen years of my sobriety, I increasingly felt that I was my own person and could follow no one. But this alternated with guilt. Deep down, I believed that I must be a "bad" AA member, since I didn't seem to be following the hard line of AA (if there even is such a thing!).

The new cutting edge of my life possessed me. I moved quickly, talked a great deal—sometimes very thoughtlessly—without saying very much, and was concurrently involved in many activities. I attended multiple AA meetings; educated health professionals; held seventy-two-hour weekend marathon groups with nurses, doctors, pharmacists, and dentists; lectured and conducted groups on addiction at San Francisco Bay Area hospitals; and handled a busy private gynecological practice.

In 1967, at the request of the dean of the School of Medicine and the chancellor of the University of California Medical Center in San Francisco, I left my private practice and became coordinator of the Allied Health Professions. I eagerly assumed my new role at the medical center, but now, in addition to all my other activities, I raced from there to San Francisco State University to San Francisco City College to Golden Gate College to the University of San Francisco, attempting to expand the educational level of their health professionals. Thank heavens my energy level was high!

For a sideline—as if I needed one!—I was one-quarter owner of a film business, Professional Arts, Inc., which produced educational films. I was medical consultant and recorded narration for its scientific and medical films, several of which dealt with addiction. I even held membership cards in SAG (Screen Actors Guild) and in AFTRA (American Federation of Television and Radio Artists).

As I look back now on those days, I wonder how I managed to stay in one piece! But I was expanding my outlook and discovering new frontiers. I gulped life in large quaffs, just as I had formerly gulped booze. I was often accused of being on a dry drunk, but I viewed my frantic activities as leading to new spiritual growth. Experience had shown me that spiritual growth arose from deep psychic pain. And goodness knows, I was in pain!

Always searching for answers and for emotional relief, I tried Gestalt therapy. I participated in Gestalt groups led by Dr. Fritz Perls at Esalen, the growth center in Big Sur, California. Fritz took me apart emotionally many times, then lovingly put me back together again. This was the hot tub, hot seat, and hippie age, a very loving era, but at times almost too much. Perhaps it was *I* who was the hippie—an aging one—and perhaps it was *I* who was too much.

There was a strange, exhilarating note of pain in virtually everything I did. I believed that these many activities were good for me. I began to see clearly how I was connected to everything and everyone. My big mistake was that I thought I could *control* it all, like a sort of demi-god. But I could not suppress the urge to run about frantically. I told myself that the aim of my rapid, and at times disjointed, activities was to experience new awareness. Sometimes my demand to control it all was clear to me; at other times it was very vague. But I seemed possessed to keep moving.

A Devoted AA Rebel
and 'the Forum'

When I'd been sober over ten years, I developed a resentment toward newcomers in AA. Strange, but true. For some reason I felt that those in middle and prolonged sobriety were being pushed aside by newcomers. I decided that a new group was needed, for old-timers and for those who disagreed with inherent religious precepts held by some AAs.

Children's Hospital in San Francisco provided a hospital conference room for an evening meeting. The new group, called 'the Forum,' first met on August 17, 1965. There were about ten of us. The group was designed to welcome mid-timers and old-timers in AA, and those who were unhappy with the religious connotations of AA's Twelve Steps. Oddly, by this time, I had become more comfortable with the words that had previously bothered me in the Twelve Steps of AA. I realized that many AA members liked and needed the religious flavor of Steps Four, Five, Six, Seven, and Eleven. Nevertheless, many others were at unrest. Some of them had decided to leave AA because they deduced, incorrectly—of course—that AA was a religious organization.

In order to entice these discontented members to hang around, I designed a ten-step program of recovery from chemical dependency for them. *We made it very clear in the Forum meetings that these Ten Steps did not replace AA's Twelve Steps.* They were for alcoholics and chemical dependents who were uncomfortable with the Twelve Steps. The rest of us used the Twelve Steps of AA.

The Forum's credo: "The Chemical Dependency Forum is designed to offer help to persons using any kind of mind-altering drugs who want sobriety. Permanent abstinence from *all* drugs is our credo. All users are welcome irrespective of their drug of choice. We feel that addiction represents a single disease with many open doors leading to it—e.g., alcohol, opiates, amphetamines, cocaine, 'uppers,' 'downers,' marijuana, etc. Our sharing motto is 'Come one, Come all.' Our precepts are pliable and may be interpreted in any way that helps an individual to maintain abstinence."

The following outlines the ten step program which agnostic and atheist recovering people could use:

Chemical Dependency Forum

1. We realize deeply that we cannot handle mind-altering drugs safely. . . our attempt to do so courts disaster.

2. As we commit ourselves to abstinence, we welcome Nature's healing process into our lives.

3. In the Forum group, we discuss our common problems in recovery; to do so hastens healing.

4. We find a friend, usually also recovering, with whom we can discuss our deepest, guarded secrets. Release and freedom become ours.

5. By making amends to ourselves and to others, we put to rest past injuries.

6. When we face our emotional problems squarely, we discover that change automatically happens. We do not seek change . . . it simply occurs.

7. Our lives are orderly and full of meaning as we live second for second—*now*.

8. Recovery together constitutes a fabric of unity. Each of us, however, follows a unique, personalized pattern of recovery.

9. We share our lives with those who are still drinking or using. Many of them decide to join us.

10. Our meeting doors are open to all users of mind-altering substances. The welcome mat is in full view.

The Forum was one of the most exciting meetings that I ever attended. An hour before the group began, Chuck G., Ted F., Johnny S., Jerry A., Ray B., Harry R., Si P., and a few others collected for dinner at the California Street Hickory Pit. Throughout the meal we laughed and heckled one another. Good fun! After dinner we walked the block to Children's Hospital and met in a conference room there.

The Forum format was somewhat different from the usual AA meeting. The secretary called the meeting to order and then announced, "At the Forum, each of you can say and do anything that you wish, providing that it does not physically hurt anyone. No hitting allowed. Speak up when you care to. No one is called on in this meeting. We do not mind silence. The Big Book of Alcoholics Anonymous is here at the head of the table, and so are the Ten Steps of Chemical Dependency, which are *not* meant to replace the Twelve Steps of AA. The Ten Steps are simply an adjunct. Use either of them as you wish."

Forum meetings were usually vigorous and stimulating. But if group energy was low and the meeting dull, we accepted and embraced that, too.

Most, but not all, Forum members were also devoted AA members. For those who were not, it was the Forum or nothing. We had no objections. Forum members were close and friendly. Some seemed to enjoy a freedom from traditional AA. The success rate in sobriety was never studied, but it seemed high to me: perhaps eighty percent sober at the end of two years. Forum members tended to be rebellious, innovative, and inventive. For example, sometimes a leader requested an hour of silence. Usually no one objected. If someone did, the leader might confront him, and the confrontation could be fiery and intense. But Forum meetings had no goals other than an opportunity to air opinions and ideas. No one was determined to be right or wrong, correct or incorrect. No medals for opinions or ideas. Members were simply given the opportunity to throw ideas into the ring and to discuss them and/or to be confronted about them—a sort of benevolent free-for-all.

Some Forum meetings were replicas of AA meetings. Again, usually no one objected; it would be like coming home, and everyone would feel good. Forum meetings lasted exactly one hour, and closed in typical AA fashion with either the Serenity Prayer or the Lord's Prayer.

After the meeting, about a dozen of us went to the Sugar Plum on California Street (across from the Hickory Pit where we'd had dinner) for pie, cake, and ice cream. One member, Joe B., had a sweetheart who was a Sugar Plum waitress. Joe wouldn't join us after the meeting because he said he "preferred not to mix business with pleasure!"

Within a month or two, the Forum grew from ten to about thirty-five or forty members. Some left and returned to AA, but visited us from time to time. Others tired of traditional AA and joined the Forum for the excitement of free, benevolent confrontation.

During the first year, a Forum splinter group formed in San Carlos, California, for people who lived on the Peninsula. Occasionally the two groups combined into a large one, but this was no deterrent to group confrontation and discussion.

Some of my happiest hours were with Forum members. Even today, over twenty years later, many of us are still close, fast friends.

In 1970 I left the San Francisco Bay Area. Eleven years later, when I returned and visited the Forum, the format and group excitement were still at a high level, but the confrontation element had subsided. The Forum was now a men's discussion group. The Ten Steps of Chemical Dependency were rarely used, but rebellious AA members still used the meeting as a refuge. I couldn't have been more pleased.

On August 17, 1985, the Forum celebrated its twentieth anniversary. About 250 Forum members attended. Not a bad turnout for a bunch of irritable AA rebels!

CONFRONTATION:
A TREND IN THE 1960S

"Role playing is a method of teaching and learning. A real-life problem, such as a disagreement between people, is described. Members of a group act out roles. Each tries different ways of behaving in the situation. Other members of the group observe the effects of the behavior. Then the group discusses what happened and often suggests other ways of handling the problem. Role playing, sometimes called sociodrama, *was perfected in the 1930s, and has been used in schools, industry, social work, and adult education. Doctors use a form of role playing, called* psychodrama, *to treat mentally ill patients. Role playing helps people understand the feelings of others. It also allows people to test new solutions to problems."*

World Book Encyclopedia

In the spring of 1967, I became active in psychodrama and sociodrama groups, under the direction of Leon Fine, Ph.D., of Portland, Oregon.

One black group member, Reggie, was a race relations activist. He lived in the Midwest but had come to Portland for more group work experience. Kindly but firmly, Reggie confronted me about my racism. My eyes were opened for the first time, and though I felt surprised and chagrined, I made no apology for my racist attitude. I had been raised and conditioned that way, as had most white people of my generation, area, and society. Now I wanted to do something if I could to improve race relations at home.

I was acquainted with Michael Murphy, owner and founder of Esalen Institute in Big Sur, California. I'd heard that he had asked Price Cobbs, M.D., George Leonard, Mike Brown, Ron Brown, Ph.D., and John Poppy to set up black-white confrontation groups.

Confrontation was a trend in the 1960s.

I signed up for a black-white confrontation marathon with Dr. Ron Brown as leader and John Poppy as co-leader. For the first several hours I remained aloof, but inwardly I was eager to learn.

After twelve hours, Ron Brown put me in the hot seat. Though kind, Ron was pushy. He had to be! In that situation, blacks and whites tended to do poorly together. Ron's purpose was to open the issue of racism, to see that it was discussed openly by both blacks and whites, and to steer the group toward a finale of co-operation and friendship. An enormous order. Ron gently carved me to pieces, but the more he confronted me, the more resistant I became and the less I said. I simply withdrew, and he advised the group to leave me alone. I crawled slowly to the sidelines, and after several hours of deep turmoil, I broke out in sobs. I felt bewildered, caught, and had no idea where to turn.

Gently Ron and John put me back together again. They had done their job. I could see that, through no fault of my own, racism was clearly a part of me. That was really all they wanted from me: a simple awareness!

At the end of the group, I was a new person. I could see the benefits of confrontation. I had the healed wounds and scars to prove it.

One evening about a week later, I was struck by an innovative notion: I decided that Alcoholics Anonymous *needed* group confrontation. So I embarked on a period of investigating the benefits of confrontation. I believed that soon I would invent *a new kind of AA group* which would "save AA" and appeal to everybody. How wrong I was!

In the meantime, Ron Brown and Mike Brown asked me to be a white leader in the black-white confrontation groups. I was complimented. I joined them eagerly (as though I had nothing else to do!) and became a good friend of Price, George, John, Mike, and Ron.

The black/white confrontation groups were active at Esalen for a year or so. One day, Philip Lee, M.D., chancellor of the University of California Medical Center in San Francisco, invited the groups to move to the campus. Since this was one of the first U.S. medical centers, if not *the* first, to accept large numbers of minority students in its schools of medicine, pharmacy, dentistry, and nursing, the chancellor hoped that the confrontation groups would help integrate blacks and whites on campus. (This proved to be only partially true.) So Price Cobbs moved the black-white confrontation groups to San Francisco, and they became very active—sometimes too active! At times, tempers were hot. Unfortunately, some of the anger and hatred expressed in these groups carried over into everyday life on campus. This proved distressing to all of us. We had been very careful at the end of each marathon to bring blacks and whites together in a modicum of mutual understanding and love—very difficult to do at best! One group on campus (mainly whites) objected strenuously to the black-white confrontations, saying that they were a disturbing element. We group leaders were surprised and disappointed. We reasoned that the objection was actually a racist outburst. This was probably correct, but—unhappily—the black-white confrontation groups were discontinued during the next year.

My experience with these confrontation groups led me to wonder if AA had missed the boat in not being confrontive enough, person to person. There was no feedback in most AA meetings that I attended. I now believed that the two- or three-minute lectures given by each person at AA meetings were limited and limiting. I decided to do something about this. I invited "special members" of Alcoholics Anonymous—people whom I believed were sufficiently open and secure to withstand confrontation—to "a new kind of group." My meeting plan included enough time for "exposed" individuals to be put back together again, and consequently to feel all right about themselves.

I dimly sensed that although the purposes of AA and of confrontation groups were similar, the techniques to reach like goals were markedly different. An important point! After all, AA is a gentle organization, in which people are loved unconditionally and encouraged to share their inner selves *when they can bring themselves to do so.* AA is *not* a therapeutic environment in which to *force* change by confrontation. At the time, it did not occur to me that while a few AA members might have welcomed a confrontive type of AA group, instituting a general confrontation modality in AA would have been very distasteful to most.

Nonetheless, I proceded to establish this new kind of AA group: first named the Floorsitters, later called SYESH.

The Floorsitters was a group of about twenty-five AA men and women who accepted my invitation to join the confrontation matrix. The group served a special purpose for me: *I* found that *I* could be more real in the confrontation atmosphere than at regular AA meetings. My covert urge at regular AA meetings was to say something brilliant rather than personal and meaningful; this attitude did not help me deal with my own issues. Some AA members tested the Floorsitters meetings and recoiled in horror. They disliked what we were up to and made no bones about telling their AA friends that we not only had deserted AA, but also had lost our minds.

Other members, however, entered into the confrontation feature with zest. I believe they gained a great deal, and I know I did. I was the leader (of course!) at each meeting, and I used my driving energy to keep the group in action. And action was truly the name of the game! The Floorsitters became a tight-knit group. Many of us continued to attend regular AA meetings, but our consensus was that *our groups* were far more effective—and in some respects, they were.

After about two years, the Floorsitters decided that we had the framework to be a new organization. We did not feel that this should replace AA, but that it could be a "para-AA" organization.

Bill and Roberta S., members of the Floorsitters, had a fine plan for the new organization. Bill had devised its name, SYESH, which was an anagram for *Share Your Experience Strength Hope.* Because the anagram had been taken from the AA Preamble, we felt connected to the Program.

I supported Bill's and Roberta's idea and yet, deep down, I began to question whether we were on the right track. I believed that our confrontation meetings offered much of value, but I missed the low-key comfort of regular AA groups. I was still attending my usual Sunday morning breakfast and Tuesday evening AA meetings. I realized that although SYESH (formerly the Floorsitters) was vigorous and effective, we had missed an important point: *change cannot be made to happen,* whether in AA or in SYESH. The ingredients of change need first to be nurtured and accepted by the one wanting it; under those conditions, change can occur. I was caught in a dichotomy of sorts, and felt a bit at odds with myself.

In any event, my participation in the SYESH meetings was about to end. In 1970, my second wife, Katie, and I decided to move to Lake Tahoe. I resigned from the University of California Medical Center. I was exhausted and needed time to withdraw, rest, and take counsel with myself.

I believed the idea of the Floorsitters/SYESH meetings was a good one and filled a valuable need. We were all sincerely earnest in our attempts to invent new ways of sharing, and of promoting intimacy and growth in sobriety. I had no regrets, then or as the years passed. I believed that recovering alcoholics could benefit more from cross-dialogue than from the short synopsis offered by each member at most of the AA meetings I attended. In the very early days of AA, with so few people at each meeting, we dialogued with one another all the time. But as AA expanded, the increasing size of most meetings made this kind of communication difficult.

I finally decided, however, that *dialogue was not confrontation.* And I still believe today that cross-dialogue and mild confrontation should be encouraged at some AA meetings, so that people can respond and relate to one another, rather than to speak one after the other to the group as a whole. Because of time constraints, such dialogue will usually prevent *all* members from speaking at each meeting, but it might help make whatever *is* said to be more intimate, thoughtful, and meaningful.

Of course, cross-dialogue *does* take place all over the world at small AA meetings, and at large meetings that are divided—sometimes for just part of the meeting—into small discussion groups. And the "formal" settings of listed AA meetings are hardly the sole option: informal meetings are held in people's homes; in restaurants, coffee shops, cafes and discos; on the job; in cars, planes, boats, and trains—anywhere that two or more AA members gather and decide to have one.

LECTURES ON SEXUALITY, ALCOHOLISM

In the late 1960s, during the Irritable Period of my sobriety, several personal events occurred in another sphere of my life which were very satisfying to me.

The first was the Jake Gimble sex lectures at the University of California Medical Center in San Francisco. I had been a fellow of the American Association of Marriage and Family Therapy for many years. While a gynecological research consultant to Dr. Alfred C. Kinsey and his group back in the 1940s, I had learned a great deal about the sex lives of average American men and women. I applied this knowledge with much success to a new dimension of my obstetrical/gynecological practice: marriage counseling, with special emphasis on sexual therapy.

The hippie movement of the 1960s had encouraged a liberal attitude toward life in America, and especially toward sex. Years before, Jake Gimble had left a legacy to pay lecturers on various aspects of American life, but particularly on human sexuality. With the stage thus set for an open public discussion of sex, in 1967 Salvatore Lucia, M.D., professor of medicine at the UC Medical Center, invited me to give the Jake Gimble sex lectures on campus in San Francisco. He suggested that I offer five weekly lectures, one-and-a-half hours long, followed by a question-and-answer period. This was a big order, but an excellent opportunity for me.

My lecture series, "Self-acceptance and Sex," viewed sex from every standpoint. The newspapers announced it and the turnout far exceeded our expectations. We filled the 800-seat Life Sciences auditorium and seated the overflow in several large medical lecture halls, transmitting the lectures to them through television monitors. I believe that the success of my Jake Gimble sex lectures stemmed from the fact that people in the San Francisco area had grown tired of sexual repression, and were hungry for a free and open discussion of such a vital activity in their lives. Fortunately, the liberal atmosphere of the 1960s—particularly in California—provided the opportunity.

The happy aura surrounding these lectures neutralized some of the tension that had been building in me. The public's enthusiasm for my lectures helped to dissipate much of the disapproval from AA traditionalists about my nonconforming AA groups. The tensions in my life eased a great deal.

Additional opportunities to educate also came my way during this time—but with a different focus.

The professor of psychiatry at the UC Medical School invited me to lecture third-year students about alcoholism. At that time, medical students received little or no education about the disease, except for a two-week observation of skid row alcoholics who were on the psychiatric ward at San Francisco General Hospital. Our medical students had deduced that *all* alcoholics were skid row types. I assured them that this was not so; that only 3 percent of alcoholics would be found on skid row, and that the majority would never even *see* skid row. I told them that this type of alcoholic was (and still is) rare, certainly *not* the kind of alcoholic that most of these students would regularly see in their future medical practices. I redefined alcoholism for them, stressing that most alcoholics still had wives, husbands, families, money, jobs, and the like.

Leading toxicologist David E. Smith, M.D., founder-director of the Haight Ashbury Free Medical Clinic in San Francisco, attended one of my lectures as a medical student in the early 1960s. He tells me that my lectures were all that he had on alcoholism in his medical education—a tragic oversight. Today's medical students get more educational exposure to addictive disease than this example. A special course on chemical dependency has been designed for this purpose.

I lost no opportunity to try to educate physicians, whether students or hospital department heads. Several San Francisco Bay Area hospitals invited me to give their department heads mild confrontation and sensitivity awareness sessions once a week in order to stimulate interdepartmental friendship. I made it a point to discuss alcoholism and other drug addiction in at least one session with my captive audience. I wanted to encourage the doctors to share attitudes about the disease. As I expected, most had punitive attitudes toward the addicted person. But, through a combination of group sharing and lectures, I made a serious attempt to show these physicians that alcoholism/drug addiction is a treatable physical disease. I explained that alcoholics and drug addicts need to be treated with warmth and compassion, not with punitive rebuffs. Some department heads accepted these facts; others demonstrated only mild interest.

I also conducted a two-day confrontation group between members of the registered nurses and the licensed vocational nurses licensing boards in Sacramento. Part was devoted to nursing care in alcoholism. I was pleased to discover that in this group, unlike the department-head physicians, most of the nurses possessed a feeling of warmth toward the recovering alcoholic/drug addict patient.

While attempting to educate health professionals, I also felt the urge to bring the story of alcoholism and recovery to the general public. I gave my Blackboard Talk on the nature of addiction and alcoholism to nonmedical organizations, including the Masons, Rotary, Kiwanis, and Lions Clubs; Catholic men's groups; the General Semantic Society; and a few small private gatherings. These lectures were rewarding for me. I usually told my drinking history and disclosed my own recovery from alcohol addiction. My answers to questions from the audience were open, direct, and—I hope—helpful.

I still lecture on alcoholism/drug addiction to private and professional groups, for I believe that the public continues to need education.

My daughter's career

▲ ▲ ▲ ▲ ▲ ▲ ▲ ▲ ▲

Another important event in my life at this time concerned my daughter Jane. Although my wife, Mary, and I were involved in separate activities in most areas of our lives, I do not believe that we had a totally dysfunctional alcoholic marriage. We were in close agreement about raising and educating Jane and did the best we could.

Delightful things were happening in Jane's life. She was (and is) a talented vocalist and operatic performer. After many years of voice study in California and in New York City, she caught the eye of Maestro Eric Langsdorf, conductor of the Boston Symphony Orchestra. He suggested that Jane enter the voice competition at Moscow's Tchaikovsky Music Festival. Prior to this, the competition had been limited to pianists, violinists, and cellists, but vocalists were included for the first time in 1966.

Musicians from all over the world gathered in Moscow for five weeks of severe competition, after which a single finalist was chosen in each category. Jane emerged the

first singer to win a gold medal. This marked the beginning of a brilliant operatic career for her.

After this singing triumph in Moscow, Jane performed all over the United States and on television and radio. She received a New York City Handel Medallion and also a Presidential Medal. She sang at the White House as a guest of President and Mrs. Lyndon B. Johnson in 1966. She made her American operatic debut at the San Francisco Opera Company, playing the leading role of Pamina in Mozart's *The Magic Flute*. That was a great success, and she sang several more times with that company, as well as with the San Francisco Symphony.

Jane decided, however, that she would benefit more and mature faster by moving to Europe. She lived and sang there for many years, only occasionally performing in the United States.

After spending a prolonged period of time with the Dusseldorf Opera Company, Jane left to become a free-lance opera singer. For the remainder of her two-decade stay in Europe, she had repeated success in countries that included Greece, Italy, France, Germany, and Austria. Vienna was her home base for her final several years in Europe. Just prior to her mother's death in April 1986, Jane decided to come home to the United States. She lives in Mill Valley, in the house where she was born, and her American operatic career is now under way.

In August 1987, Mickey and I heard Jane sing near San Francisco with a string quartet. I had last heard my daughter sing at the Salzburg Festival in Austria ten years before. As I listened now to her powerful, fully mature voice, and then watched her receive a standing ovation, tears sprang to my eyes. Afterwards, we hugged one another for the first time in years.

Jane is a strong, beautiful, talented woman, who had the inner resources to face the world, essentially alone, and become successful. My love for her is boundless.

Two Loners and
a Brief Second Marriage

My divorce from Mary had relieved me. I felt free—as if an umbilical cord had been cut—yet I also felt the loss. Divorce is not easy after over thirty years of marriage. I vacillated between feeling free of a burden and wishing that it could have been otherwise. I was at odds with myself—emotionally disheveled and deeply distracted.

Unlike some AA members, I had prolonged periods of Irritability and Inventiveness. I needed a rest—time for reflection. I stepped up my attendance at AA meetings. I also participated in several encounter and sensitivity awareness groups, which were in vogue in the 1960s.

At one of these encounter marathons in Bolinas, I met Katie, a young woman who seemed to be her own person, not given to small talk, and ready to handle anything. She was very bright—a Phi Beta Kappa—and musical, a former concert pianist. Katie and I continued our relationship after the encounter group. Our attraction to each other increased, and within a year we were married. Soon after that, we moved to Lake Tahoe.

Several months prior to our marriage, I had met Carlton Sedgeley. He owned the Royce Carlton Agency in New York City, which booked educators and artists for appearances on American university campuses. The university lecture circuit was large, and Carlton Sedgeley had no difficulty scheduling his clients. He had heard of my successful Jake Gimble sex lectures and offered to book me for similar lectures at campuses throughout the country. I signed a contract with him; he prepared a stylish brochure, and before long I was traveling from one university to the next.

For long intervals, Katie was alone in our Lake Tahoe house—hardly an enviable situation for a bride! As would be expected, trouble developed between us, and one day, Katie abruptly moved to Stinson Beach. She said she wanted to be near people and to take advantage of cultural opportunities in the San Francisco Bay Area. Reluctantly I followed her to Stinson Beach, but we lived in houses a half mile apart. Certainly a strange marriage! Shortly thereafter, Katie and I separated and she filed for a divorce. We only lived together for a few months, in two attempts. We were essentially two lone wolves who did our own thing—even while married.

From Pain to Exhilaration

Though sobriety is wonderful and a glorious way to live, it does not guarantee a trouble-free life! But, as I review the dismal periods, I can say with certainty that the pain of those days served as a preamble to the beautiful things that followed.

Through an old friend, Virginia McNamara, M.D., the dental school at the Medical College of Georgia invited me to give a sex lecture series on their Augusta campus in 1969. While there, I met William Scoggins, M.D., chairman of the Department of Obstetrics and Gynecology, and my life took an unexpected turn.

Dr. Scoggins told me that the U.S. State Department, through the American Medical Association, had arranged with several medical schools to loan medical consultants to the University of Saigon in South Vietnam. The Medical College of Georgia had agreed to send obstetricians and gynecologists, but Dr. Scoggins had been unable to find anyone willing to spend an unlimited time in Saigon.

Dr. Scoggins asked me if I would accept a professorship in his department, then consider moving permanently to Saigon in order to help upgrade the Department of Obstetrics and Gynecology at the University of Saigon Medical School.

I was stunned, but intrigued. I accepted!

I returned, elated, to the San Francisco Bay Area.

This unique turn of events marked the beginning of my Insight Period in AA. My Irritable and Inventive Periods did not subside quickly—in fact, they were mixed together almost into a single unit—but my debilitating emotional intensity began to decrease.

Five weeks before my return to Augusta, I sat alone one evening in my beautiful Sausalito, California, apartment. Each expensive painting, unique furnishing, and rare art object had an attached memory. As I gazed out a large picture window at the beauty of San Francisco Bay, I was suddenly aware of a strange, new sensation: I felt that *none* of my apartment belongings were mine! A very strange feeling indeed. I sat there all evening, caught up in this feeling that I did not own the very things that I had selected and paid for. I couldn't understand it.

The feeling remained the next morning. So, I reasoned, why not sell my belongings? I had planned to store everything while I was in Saigon. Instead I called a San Francisco auction center and described what I had to sell. They offered to collect my things the following week.

I felt a walking-on-air exhilaration. I attended many AA meetings in the next few days. My mood of excitement must have radiated from me. Friends said, "I don't know what's come over you, but I hope you don't lose it. You've been so glum for a long, long time."

A few days later, returning from a walk, a stranger stopped me. "Are you Dr. M.?" he asked. I didn't know him, but nodded slowly. He smiled and said, "Rumor has it that you're leaving the area for an overseas assignment. Is that correct?"

I looked at him rather tentatively before finally confirming that the rumor was true. "But," I asked, "how did you discover that?"

He replied that secrets were difficult to hide in a small town. "My reason for approaching you is to ask what plans you have for disposing of the beautiful furniture in your apartment."

I stared at him in amazement. "Have you been in my apartment?" I couldn't believe that he had—I didn't know him.

He shook his head. "No, but I live 'way up there on the mountain, and I have a telescope. I can look down through your big bay windows and see the beautiful things that you own." Before

I could respond he continued, "What are you going to do with all your furniture and pictures when you leave?"

I explained about the San Francisco auctioneer. The stranger asked if he could put in a bid for my things, and I replied, "Perhaps so."

He seemed like a rather straightforward, honest individual, so I was more bewildered than frightened. I escorted him to my front door. As soon as he entered my apartment, he exclaimed, "Oh my goodness, I can't afford *these* things."

Then I realized that I might have found a buyer on *my* terms: if I offered him a *low* enough price, he might buy everything and allow me to continue using my furniture until the day I left. Whereas if I sold everything to the auctioneers, I would have to live in an empty home during my final weeks in Sausalito. We sat down. I mentioned a ridiculously low price for everything in the apartment. I hoped that he would snap it up because he seemed so eager. And indeed he did! He wrote me a check on the spot, and he readily agreed that I could use my belongings until I departed for Augusta.

The day I left California, I dropped my keys on the kitchen counter, walked out the apartment door, and left without the slightest urge to look back. I walked away from my furniture, my pictures, my clothes—shirts, socks, shoes—my television, and my hi-fi equipment. I even left first editions of the Big Book and of *Twelve Steps and Twelve Traditions,* both inscribed by Bill W. I abandoned my entire medical library—obstetrics, gynecology, psychiatry, marital counseling. My tax records all went into a dumpster. I closed all my bank accounts and took the money with me. I packed just enough clothes to get me across the country to Georgia. I felt lighter than ever before in my whole life. I was exhilarated by *leaving everything* of mine *behind.* Now I was unburdened.

I drove away from Sausalito on a cloud, feeling at one with the universe. The year was 1969. I was free, in solitude, and eagerly anticipating my experience at the medical school in Augusta, followed by my Saigon trip.

En route to Georgia, I attended an AA meeting in a different city almost every day. I felt as though I had come home.

I also visited my good friends Bill Masters and Ginny Johnson, of the Masters and Johnson Institute, in St. Louis. (Pioneers in the scientific study of sexual arousal and the treatment of sexual problems, William H. Masters, M.D., and Virginia E. Johnson wrote the best-selling *Human Sexual Response,* published in 1966.)

During my cross-country automobile trip, I reviewed the previous decade and realized that I had been driven—demanding much of myself as well as of others. The AA slogans "Easy Does It," "First Things First," and "Live and Let Live" had dropped out of my sight. I had been peripherally aware of the slogans, but they had become simply words. Yet I could also see that I had needed to live through those periods, be they tense, irritable, joyous, or happy. Once they had spent themselves, an emotional mutation occurred and I became a new person in a different place.

On the trip east, I thought a great deal about my friend George H., who had first acquainted me with the Four I's of recovery. I began to see that the last several years had been a combination of irritability and inventiveness—which had led me to found the Forum, the Floorsitters, SYESH, and the like. I had never really expected to experience any of the Four I phases personally, but—in fact—I had! For the moment, however, I was in a peaceful, pleasant place. I was glad to be on my way to Southeast Asia. I felt as though I was leaving many of my troubles behind.

There are those who might see this as a geographic cure for the restlessness of a recovering alcoholic, but in my opinion I was running away from nothing. I believe that my experiences simply happened to me. Although some of my troubles had diminished by virtue of my insights, the heat and emotional intensity had not totally evaporated. Nonetheless, I was aware of a new inner relaxation, and I felt grateful for it.

I moved into a temporary furnished apartment in Augusta, eager to get to work. I returned with zest to the operating room and found my fingers as nimble as ever. Within a few weeks I learned a great deal about the Medical College of Georgia and how it functioned. Dr. McNamara had AA friends in Augusta; during my three months there, I attended an AA meeting almost every night. The meetings were soothing and a very welcome relief from my last few frantic, but sober, years.

Finally I was ready. With appropriate good-byes to my new friends at the medical school, I left for New York City en route to Saigon. In recent years I had drifted away from the people in the AA General Service Office because I had been feeling so irritable, and so involved in a multitude of inventive activities. However, I spent several days in New York in order to renew friendships. AA's General Service Office was decorated and furnished better than before; the staff who worked there seemed more together. I had a good time because I felt free and light.

I caught a plane for Dusseldorf, Germany. I had not seen my daughter, Jane, for several years, and we spent a lovely few days together in Dusseldorf. I arrived in time to catch her performance in Mozart's *Cosi Fan Tutte.* She was outstanding and very professional.

On the flight to Saigon by way of Hong Kong, I became aware of a deep ache in my heart. I had discussed the need for "serenity" with Bill and several staff members at GSO in New York. I could see that my own serenity was actually rather thin, and I yearned for a more substantial one. In the weeks that followed, I developed a burning, driving search for serenity which led to another stressful period in my life. I went through more inner turmoil, but my experiences in Southeast Asia finally pushed open the door of Insight. This led to a new level of what Alcoholics Anonymous—as a matter of fact, all living—is really about!

INSIGHT IN AA

THE INSIGHT PERIOD

My Insight Period has no boundaries, since new insights have occurred continuously throughout my sobriety.

Some insights that were important to me during this period were:

- ▲ Realizing that we in AA are all human beings who are joyfully struggling to understand sobriety.

- ▲ The slogans "First Things First," "Live and Let Live," and "Easy Does It" becoming a part of my being.

- ▲ My self-respect building as I recognized that I have the right to be who I am and to practice the AA Program as I see fit.

- ▲ Recognizing that my internal and external lives are the same.

- ▲ Self-demands and self-hatred diminishing as my personal appreciation expanded. Realizing that as one loves oneself, so will one love one's neighbors. Seeing that when I debase others I simply reflect my own view and, therefore, debase myself. Self-doubt and self-hatred can be easily projected onto others; we then find fault with them and are in conflict with them. In my Insight phase, I learned that the conflict was not so much with my neighbors as it was an essential struggle within myself. This insight was painful, but it was also honest, straight, clear, and paved the way for me to achieve inner quiet. After all, for me the only successful revolution takes place *within;* no amount of *external manipulation* will do the job.

▲The diminishing sense of being a follower of others. I began to appreciate living in divine solitude. In a sense, *each of us is the world . . . our version of the world.* Knowing this, I began to relax inside and simply watch my life happen. As I looked at others, I realized that I am really observing myself. I began to treat others as I would want to be treated.

Irritability and even inventiveness have persisted throughout my sobriety, although their frequency and intensity seem to diminish with time.

Awareness and insight usually grow out of pain and struggle. With each insight, I find my egocentricity diminishes and a glad embracing of the world follows. To embrace the world is to embrace ourselves. My own insight has grown in jagged leaps and bounds as the following personal experiences occurred.

A LOVE AFFAIR WITH SAIGON

"The more I traveled throughout the world with AA at my side, the more my sobriety grew."

Dr. Earle M.

As I arrived in the beautiful, magical city of Saigon in 1970, the issue of my thin serenity temporarily receded into the background. Norman Hoover, M.D., director of the USAID Project, met me at the Saigon Airport. USAID—United States Aid for International Development—provided educational, financial, and medical aid abroad and included the American contingent of visiting medical professors. Through Dr. Hoover, the University of Saigon Medical School was connected to several American medical schools that supplied specialists. Dr. Hoover was enthusiastic and robust, with a pleasing demeanor and very kind eyes. I felt instantly at home with him. He loved Saigon and, I believe, would have liked to remain there. In time I, too, began to feel that way. There was talk about updating the Hue Medical School, in the northern section of South Vietnam. The Hue Medical School would have needed a USAID program, and some of us hoped that we could transfer there. But the fall of South Vietnam made that hope impossible.

As Dr. Hoover drove me from the Saigon Airport to the USAID No. 1 building, I was aware that the face of Saigon, once called the "Pearl of the Orient," was now etched and torn by the ravages of war. But it was still beautiful to me.

The city was crowded with people. Until the Vietnam War, Saigon accommodated about three-quarters of a million people. Now, with the constant trickle of Vietnamese into the city, the population had swelled to three and a half million. It was jammed! The war-weary Vietnamese police had great difficulty controlling the traffic—mainly bicycles and small motorcycles.

My first morning, when I stepped outside, I was absolutely entranced by the sounds, smells, traffic, strange colors, and tiny rows of stores/sheds crammed between beautiful French colonial buildings. I was overwhelmed and excited, like a kid in a candy store. I loved Saigon—for that matter, all of Asia—so much that after I'd been there for several months, some University of Saigon Medical School faculty members told me, "Your interest in us and in our city indicates that you are most likely a 'reincarnated Vietnamese.' "

For the first six weeks I lived at USAID No. 1, a six-story building in the heart of Saigon. USAID No. 1 resembled a second-class American hotel. The rooms were small but adequate. A restaurant was located on the first floor, with beautiful Chinese and Vietnamese waitresses who spoke English reasonably well. The cooking was distinctly American. For Vietnamese or Chinese cooking, one had to eat elsewhere, and there was plenty of opportunity to do just that.

I had my first real taste of Vietnamese home cooking when I rented a one-bedroom apartment in the center of Saigon's tiny downtown section. A well-to-do Vietnamese family owned the apartment complex. A wonderful cook/maid called Ba Phep came with the apartment. Although "Ba Phep" meant "Mrs. Cook" in English, Ba Phep insisted that this was her real name; I didn't argue the point. I was happy to hire her, and I maintained an apartment for her and her five children elsewhere in the complex. I don't believe that I have ever been treated so gently and thoughtfully as I was by Ba Phep and her family. Her cooking (both Vietnamese and American) was the best I had ever tasted. She shopped for me, cooked breakfast and supper, did my laundry, and treated me like a king. Her five children helped with the housework. They were a close-knit group and made me a part of their family. I admired them immensely. My contact with them was a joyous one.

All USAID personnel were assigned automobiles with chauffeurs. Mine was Ba Soung, a wiley, alert Vietnamese woman, who spoke English. She was rather suspicious of Americans. And yet she became loyal and devoted to me. I, in turn, admired her. For many years Ba Soung—who was very poor—had lived solely by her wits. She drove me on my daily hospital rounds and waited for me faithfully, no matter how long I was occupied. She also taught me to speak a little Vietnamese. I never mastered the tones of the language, but Ba Soung understood my American-accented attempts. After all, *she* had taught me! She loved to have me talk in Vietnamese. I could have asked her to do things in English, because she understood both languages, but to hear *me* speak her native tongue made her chuckle. Through Ba Soung, Ba Phep, and others, I came to admire and love the Vietnamese people. Though I visited and enjoyed Hong Kong, Bangkok, Taipei, Singapore, Katmandu, and numerous cities in India—and even in Iran—nothing approached my deep love for Saigon. It simply hypnotized me.

On one of my "R and R" trips in 1971 I spent two weeks in Iran. The shah was still ruler. I lectured at the medical school on the cultural aspects of alcoholism and on sexuality, and was asked to consider a professorship in obstetrics and gynecology. I chose not to accept the offer.

While in Iran I attended an AA meeting. Alcohol is forbidden in this country, but apparently it can be found! Five Iranians were in that group of twenty AA members. Like most other Middle and Far Eastern AA meetings, this one had a different spiritual dimension than American meetings. The fundamental AA philosophy was similar, but the word "God" was not used. Instead, "Mohammed," "Allah," "Buddha," "Krishna," and "Rama" replaced the word "God" in the Twelve Steps. Actually, Southeast Asians and many Middle Easterners were rather critical of the Christian religions. They said their dislike for them was because

Christianity fostered "horrible feelings of guilt." This, they believed, failed to offer Divine support. But I was not disturbed by their criticisms because my Insight into AA living was at a high point. I was preoccupied with the novel excitement of discovering and experiencing differences between the world's religions. I found it fascinating, that although various religions were in some discord, an inherent harmony existed between all of them. Each in its own way described God or Allah or Krishna, and the nature of Heaven or Enlightment or Nirvana. These departures from Christianity interested me and they strengthened my sobriety in a strange way. The more I traveled throughout the world with AA by my side, the more my sobriety grew.

The little AA meeting in Saigon was a godsend. Twice a week, a group of twelve to fifteen Americans and two Vietnamese met in a small Catholic church in the center of Saigon. American AA members came and went. Many were military personnel on temporary duty from the South Pacific. Others were contract people in various professions. People who travel the world exhibit a strange, rebellious freedom. Even Americans exhibit a new kind of exhilaration outside the confines of the United States. The home ties that bind have been broken, and they feel free. Consequently our Saigon AA meetings were brisk and vibrant, and I loved them.

Internal and external moods merge

▲ ▲ ▲ ▲ ▲ ▲ ▲ ▲ ▲

A proper description of my growing insight in Alcoholics Anonymous must include some of my experiences and moods in Saigon, as well as in other parts of Southeast Asia. I made several trips around the world on rest-and-relaxation periods, visiting AA on every continent. I attended meetings of AA in India (especially in Bombay), in Indonesia (Jokarta), in Singapore (seafaring men who met in the YMCA), in Hong Kong, Taipei, Iran, and later in Peru (Lima), Ecuador, Panama, Mexico (Mexico City and Cuernavaca), and in every province of Canada.

But my Insight Period is intimately entwined with my experiences in Asia, which equated directly with my inner awareness. So, as I describe my travels and encounters, I am, at the same time, describing my growing inner awareness. I had previously considered external experiences and internal moods to be separate. But I discovered to my delight that for me they are, in fact, essentially the same, and that the two together describe who I am at any given moment. This discovery was important in my Insight Period.

Sober in a Chinese Opium Den!

"Alcoholics are not safe from relapse even after ten, fifteen or twenty years of sobriety, unless they continue to use the tools they acquired in treatment."

L. Ann Mueller, M.D., and **Katherine Ketcham,**
Recovering: How to Get and Stay Sober

The more I saw and learned, the more I believed that if enough of the AA philosophy invaded me, the taking of alcohol or other drugs would become impossible. Here is a story to prove that point.

Being an avid walker, I came to know Saigon like the palm of my hand. In Cholon, a section of the city reserved for the Chinese, I became acquainted with a young Chinese shopkeeper. I would stop in his store for a Coca-Cola on my daily walks. He spoke enough Vietnamese so we could exchange greetings, and we became very friendly over the months. One day, explaining that he was to marry his childhood sweetheart, he invited me to his bachelor party.

The party was held in a Chinese opium den! About fifty Chinese men were present—I was the sole Caucasian. We were each assigned a Chinese prostitute. Sexual activity was expected in small, bedded cubicles off the den, but my assignee got drunk and passed out (just my luck!). Booze and drugs such as marijuana, hashish, and smokeable Persian heroin were in plentiful supply. Also nearby were cases of bourbon, Scotch, gin, and vodka.

One game at this Chinese bachelor party (as at American bachelor parties) was to see how fast guests could chug-a-lug alcohol. The bridegroom was most frequently on the spot. The rule was that he must drink quickly while the guests counted "one, two, three, four," etc., in Chinese.

I entered the game with an empty glass. A Chinese man objected. He was drunk, and irritated that my glass wasn't *full*.

Now I was on the spot. I could easily have engaged in drinking or taking drugs, and no one involved in my sober life would have known the difference. *But the AA philosophy had penetrated me deeply. Not only would I not drink, but I could not!* AA and sobriety were the most important things in my life. The participants at this party knew nothing about AA or alcoholism. I couldn't explain my position because of the language barrier. What to do?

I wanted to imply that booze made me ill and that therefore I could not drink. Finally I thought of the game of *charades*. I pretended to drink from my empty glass. I pointed to my abdomen, crouched, and pretended to vomit. My charade was successful: the leader of the group gave me a glass of water instead of alcohol. But I even refused to drink this, suspicious that someone might fill the glass with gin or vodka masquerading as water. Using more charades, I eventually made the group see that I would use only an empty glass. Reluctantly but politely the group allowed this courtesy.

The party lasted until dawn. Everyone was loud and drunk. Musing that bachelor parties are the same the world over, I left around 6:00 A.M. for home. My relief was indescribable. I had passed my personal acid test regarding drinking and drugs: Alcoholics Anonymous was so much a part of me that I simply could not drink!

I related my experience at our Saigon AA meeting the next Sunday. My story encouraged some of our members whose sobriety was rather shaky. They knew through my ordeal that a time might come when they, too, could not drink. We talked about that bachelor party rather frequently at our AA meetings, and it did all of us a lot of good.

Vietnamese Lessons in Life

Though I felt free and delightfully alone for the first time in my life, I was still irritable and uncertain about many facets of living. Gerry Wasserwald, M.D., a young, eager, and very competent obstetrician/gynecologist, was one of my colleagues. By the time I arrived in Saigon, Gerry had already been there for several years. After his military discharge from the army, he was to join the USAID teaching staff through the Medical College of Georgia.

My arrival must have been difficult for Gerry. We were wary of one another at first. I was older and more experienced in terms of years, but Gerry was more experienced in terms of the area. He was patient and he took great pains to see that I felt welcome and at home. We became fast friends. He sensed that I was in a crucial period of my life; he knew just when to leave me alone, when to invite me to dinner, when to advise me, and when to comfort me.

Gerry and I worked out a way of being on call for the Vietnamese medical residents. He explained their system of medical rounds, the manner in which the Vietnamese medical residents were lectured and quizzed, and in general what was expected of me. I listened intently, continually amazed at the wisdom and knowledge of this young physician whose friendship was a godsend to me. Today Gerry practices obstetrics and gynecology in southern California, and our friendship is as fresh and meaningful as it was in Saigon; we touch base with each other regularly.

My medical duties in Saigon were complex and involved two hospitals: Tu Du and Nguyen Van Hoc. Because of Saigon's dense population, the patient load was enormous. We established several operating teams so that we could work around the clock. About 150 babies were delivered every day by midwives. Gerry and I, with the obstetrical and gynecological residents, cared for the obstetrical complications and supervised all the gynecological surgery.

I had learned a great deal about close interpersonal relations in AA, but that was nothing compared to the personal intimacies that I observed on the obstetrical units. At the Tu Du hospital, a large labor room accommodated about eighty beds, always full. I noticed that each bed contained *two,* and sometimes *three,* women, all in labor, all comforting one another. At first I thought my eyes were deceiving me. The women massaged, held, and were very tender with each other. I could not imagine this occurring in a United States hospital. Although Vietnam was considered to be a developing nation, it was a superior nation in an interpersonal sense. Its people possessed an eager willingness to relate to those around—far superior to the questionable willingness that I had grown accustomed to in the United States. In Saigon, Insight into the longing that human beings feel for one another warmed my heart.

My counterparts at the University of Saigon Medical School were Nguyen Van Hong, M.D., and Nguyen Noc Giep, M.D., both professors of obstetrics and gynecology. Both were competent, open, friendly, and spoke English well. They could not have made me feel more welcome. They seemed grateful for the help offered by the American physicians and eager to use our medical/surgical principles and to let us teach their Vietnamese residents. (They are both practicing medicine in eastern United States today.)

My great joy was working with forty obstetrical and gynecological resident students. Most were women (the men were at war). They spoke English reasonably well, their fingers were nimble, and they learned American surgical techniques quickly and easily. The large number of gynecological and complicated obstetrical cases made it easy to teach these eager medical students a variety of surgical approaches.

The personal grace of the Vietnamese residents was a true phenomenon. Sometimes they were painfully polite and agreeable. While they found it difficult to share deep feelings with Americans, they listened avidly and asked questions freely. I told them about my problems learning surgical techniques in my own obstetrical and gynecological residency. This kind of sharing was a sort of Twelfth Stepping "in all my affairs" (at my work and outside of AA). The residents responded with warmth, and so did I. I sometimes wondered if they weren't, in a sense, Twelfth Stepping me!

I learned a great lesson about life from one of my residents, Tran thi Minh Chow. Our mutual deep regard was filled with unspoken affection. In a sense I fell in love with Chow, although our relationship amounted only to a gentle contact. I kissed her only once: when we said good-bye.

My job as American co-chief in the Department of Obstetrics and Gynecology included some administration. I was used to the compulsive American method of medical functioning, and unprepared for the easy-going Vietnamese style. One day I became very irritable because the medical paperwork had fallen behind; nothing seemed to be happening as I felt it should. I was alone in my office, grumbling out loud, when I felt a presence. Standing in the doorway was Tran thi Minh Chow—a ninety-pound, gorgeous Vietnamese woman. She was in her final year of residency, a competent surgeon and diagnostician, and a genuinely sweet person.

I caught her eye and the impact on me was electric. She was not critical nor playing a man-woman game. Instead she was quietly watching me fume. I gazed at her intently for several minutes. Her beautiful eyes radiated acceptance and love. After an interlude of silence as we looked into one another's eyes, I said softly, "You mean, Chow, that it's all right, don't you?" Without changing expression, she slowly nodded. Intrigued, I continued to gaze at her for a longer interval. And then I murmured, "You mean that it's *all* all right, don't you, Chow?" Again she nodded.

From that delightful twenty-five-year-old Vietnamese student I learned one of the major answers to life: *It's all all right, no matter what is happening!*

To me, this was the Third Step of AA in action. Chow was telling me that if I trusted life, and consequently myself, everything would be all right. Without knowing it, Chow added immeasurably to my insight into Alcoholics Anonymous and into living. I shall always be indebted to her.

MY SEARCH FOR SERENITY

". . . For weeks, months, perhaps years, your search took you to many places, meetings, authorities, and books, along many promising paths. Although you didn't know it then, the search itself was the root of your trouble! . . ."

E. M., Hazard, Kentucky, "Search for Cloud Nine,"
AA Grapevine, April 1977

Despite feeling progressively better, at times I still felt lost and miserable. I read sections from *Alcoholics Anonymous* and the *Grapevine* daily, and regularly attended AA meetings, all of which were of enormous help. However, en route to Saigon from New York, I had discovered a burning need to *find serenity.* I had arrived in Saigon feeling quite free, but soon after that I became preoccupied with my search for serenity. My search did not interfere with my day-to-day activities, or with my work, but nevertheless it remained uppermost in my mind.

And this after almost twenty years of sobriety!

I was still recovering from my divorces from Mary and Katie. Sometimes I wondered if I lacked the aptitude to establish a durable, loving relationship. Although most of the inner wars in me were over, I still had a long way to go. I had learned long ago that deep, intense pain inevitably preceded an emotional or spiritual discovery. I knew that some kind of growth—as yet unclear—was occurring within me. I had begun to discover some insights which were healing: I had shed my material possessions (in California) and many of my inner psychological demands. By serendipity, I had "turned over" many of my demands on life to a New Entity, which seemed to know how I needed to live. This was essentially AA's Third Step—yet the demand for serenity still held me in a tight grip. All I knew was that I *needed* it. I hoped that I would find serenity in my AA readings, or perhaps in AA meetings. I thought that I might find serenity in my little Saigon office, or in teaching residents, or in lecturing midwives, or in long hours in surgery. I believed that if I only searched hard enough, the door to serenity could open at any moment.

Southeast Asia where I lived was at the center of Hinduism, Buddhism, Confucianism, Zen Buddhism, Taoism, and ancestor worship. Would they offer me serenity, or at least a way to find it? I wondered. I decided to try them all on for size. Luong, a male resident, loaned me the book *Siddhartha* (in English) by Herman Hesse. I had read it before and I realized that young Luong was telling me: "You must be who you are. You must live your life the way you live it. There is no other choice. You, like Siddhartha, have chosen the hard path. Don't give up."

Perhaps I learn more slowly than most AA members, perhaps not—but I finally devised a plan: I would travel to the religious centers in Asia. I hoped that maybe there I would find serenity.

During periods away from Saigon, I traveled to many areas of Asia—searching and seeking, seeking and searching for the illusory and elusive serenity.

I traveled through Bali and Jakarta in Indonesia. I spent many days in Hong Kong, Singapore, Taipei (Taiwan), Bangkok (Thailand), Katmandu (Nepal), Madras, Bombay, and New Delhi in India. At times I felt like a wandering East Asian monk, for I was determined to look into the ancient religions of the Far East, to see if they would offer me serenity. I prayed and meditated in countless temples throughout Southeast Asia, hoping each time that if I meditated in the lotus position, or memorized and quoted Sanskrit prayers, or read the writings of Patanjali and bits from the Vedas, that *now* perhaps serenity would be mine. My lotus position was very awkward. The temples and their countless candles and bells intrigued and entranced me, but serenity continued to escape me.

I visited Sri Ramana Maharishi's ashram during the feast of Dewali (personal renewal), a holiday similar to Easter. We were wakened at 3:00 A.M. and were herded into a very large room containing five enormous vats in strategic locations, each filled with warm oiled water. A follower of Ramana Maharishi stood on a platform near each vat, ladled oiled water into buckets, and handed one to each of us. We went to a small washroom, washed our bodies with the warm oil-and-water mixture, and dressed in clean clothes. The washing symbolized discarding old habits, and donning new clothes—the assumption of a new character, one that is alive and spiritually very awake.

Next we took an eight-mile trek around Arunachal, the mountain. Some were barefoot. Others wore shoes. (I was one of the latter!) Slowly and prayerfully we walked around Arunachal, yelling "Rama, Rama, Rama" from time to time. We had been told that if Rama, the Hindu God, was "truly summoned" in our walk, he would rise out of the mountain and greet us. By about the sixth mile I was so exhausted that I think I saw Rama seven or eight times! I had no idea what Rama looked like, but in my fatigue I'm certain that I saw him. Actually it seemed rather comical.

I also spent time at the ashram of Sri Aurobindo, in the small French town of Pondicherry on the west coast of southern India. No fees were expected: I was invited merely to meditate and "drink in" the atmosphere. Reputedly Sri Aurobindo lived the last years of his life with his faithful partner, "The Mother," in one room, both in deep meditation and in samadhi (a state of being at complete oneness with the universe). While there, I visited nearby Oroville, the uncompleted city where praying and meditation were to be brought into harmony with the tasks of ordinary living.

I spent a week or two at these Indian ashrams, and while they were unique and invigorating experiences, serenity still eluded me.

Later, while living in Hazard, Kentucky, I described my search in an article written for the April 1977 AA Grapevine:

". . . remember how you got hold of new books that offered answers? You devoured every word, hoping to recapture the lost peace. You assumed new roles, hoping to learn new ways that would bring peace. Sometimes you acted the clown, sometimes the wise man, sometimes the aggressor, sometimes the shy violet who sat in the back row at a meeting [an AA meeting].

"Remember how you prayed more (or prayed less), or went to more AA meetings (or fewer), or went to church (or stopped going to church). A thousand things you did trying to recapture Cloud Nine and the sense of peace that had once filled you [when you were a newcomer].

"In spite of your hidden misery, you felt grateful to be sober (a long time now), but the frantic search for serenity kept driving you. Each and every thing you found and tried did help for a while—but only for a while. You just couldn't hold on to the good feelings for long; they were elusive; they slipped easily through your fingers, and sooner or later the misery returned!

"So you picked up the pace. You found and read more new books, tried on more new ideas, searched harder, became more determined to recapture bliss. (Or did you call it happiness, or serenity, or peace, or God, or truth, or beauty, or a Higher Power? It really doesn't matter.)

"The harder you searched for serenity, the worse you felt. Sober, yes. But inwardly at war. And somehow you seemed to know that this new obsession was splitting you apart. . . ."

For months I read books on Hinduism, Buddhism, Taoism, Confucianism, and ancestor worship. I visited scores of exquisite Hindu and Buddhist temples, with incense burning on altars and a sacred mood of mystery everywhere. I sat and sat with my knees crossed, as prayerful as I could be. I repeated mantras over and over. And I read portions of *Alcoholics Anonymous* and the *Grapevine* every day, and attended AA regularly. *I did it all* for two years during periods of time spent away from my work, and I still did not find serenity.

". . . One day you found yourself alone, maybe in your room, maybe walking down the street, in a restaurant, at a meeting—it doesn't really matter. You were crying and couldn't keep back the tears. You were ashamed, but you felt depressed, in shreds, blown totally apart. Never had you felt so bad. You hated everything, sometimes even AA members!

"You prayed that you would die—now. Life simply wasn't worth it! In spite of sobriety, you knew that you just couldn't keep going. Your search for peace had taken you everywhere, but you hadn't found it. Peace, maybe, wasn't to be yours, and that made life worthless, useless. Your crying broke into sobs.

"Remember how you slumped into a chair, or fell onto your bed exhausted, sick to death of everything, deeply despising your life. How you hated it!

"You relaxed a little and just lay there beaten, wanting to die.

"And then a strange thing happened. The obsession seemed to fade away. The urge to desperately try subsided. The deep need to find answers dropped away. Only a stillness remained.

"As you lay there, inwardly quiet but emotionally beaten by your own hand, having stopped searching for anything or trying anything, a deep sense of peace filled you. Serenity and bliss returned. How this had happened, you didn't know.

"But the reason didn't really matter. You didn't have to know the why of everything. Feeling serene was no longer a goal. Looking for peace was over. Somehow, you had given up. And you felt peaceful!

"A light began to dawn, and you said to yourself, 'This is another bottom, just like the one I felt years ago when I knew I was a drunk.' And this thought came to you over and over again. It penetrated deep into your heart and soul.

"Remember, as you lay there, another light dawned, and a question slowly took form in your mind:

" 'Is my real home here at the bottom? Are the bottom, peace, serenity, Cloud Nine, and the top all the same thing?' Strange new idea.

"But somehow you didn't really care whether that question was answered or not. Looking, searching, and waiting had ended.

"Remember how a wonderful drowsiness came over you as you left all those questions to be answered by someone else. If they ever could be answered. It no longer mattered to you.

"Finally, your body relaxed and you fell deeply asleep. Your first sleep in a long, long time. And you didn't know it, but you had fallen asleep with a big wide grin on your face."

Suddenly and unexpectedly, my search for serenity ended. I returned to my Saigon apartment one afternoon feeling exhausted and emotionally drained. My knees buckled, and I sank to the cool tile floor. I lay there quietly, feeling emotionally and psychologically beaten. I said to myself, The hell with serenity!

And then it happened! My desire to find serenity vanished, and I became utterly serene!

The trouble had been the search! My very search for serenity—my demand that it *be* there—had, in fact, kept serenity at a distance. When I was forced to give up the search from sheer exhaustion, serenity became mine. It had always been available to me, but my demands and my ceaseless search for it had stood in the path of my recognizing it.

I have no idea how we should handle the search for serenity, except to search until we are thoroughly beaten. As I lay on my floor that day in Saigon, I realized that I was totally defeated, and yet *now* serenity was mine. I had hit another bottom. I wondered if the "AA bottom" that we discuss so often in the Program is, therefore, really the "top?" A total paradox. This was the First Step of AA all over again, with the focus on emotional and spiritual life rather than on alcohol—defeat preceding success! I have experienced repeated emotional bottoms like this one.

Since that day, the urge to seek serenity has never returned to me. I have had more difficulties and new experiences in my life, but not in conjunction with any search for serenity.

Seeking serenity and finding nothing but exhaustion was also responsible for the dawning of AA's Third Step within me. In that Step, we "turn our will and our lives over . . ." to something else, namely to a God as we understand Him. I could not accept this premise in my life until I could prove the value of the Third Step in my *real* world. I wonder how many other AA members have had a similar experience with the Third Step?

Many of us in AA are on a constant search for emotional comfort. We are disappointed when it remains beyond our reach. For me, *the trouble was the search!* When I abandoned the search, the pain dissolved and was replaced by varying degrees of emotional comfort.

Acceptance and change

▲ ▲ ▲ ▲ ▲ ▲ ▲ ▲ ▲

In this book I have made a basic distinction between the emotional/spiritual world and the material/technological world. Because the words "emotional" and "spiritual" mean fundamentally the same thing to me, I use them interchangeably.

In the material world, technology changes rapidly. Time—past, present, and future—is a necessary ingredient of this. With new technological entities continually being devised to improve our future-oriented world, the future is very important to all of us.

But to me the emotional/spiritual world is entirely different: here there is no concept of time because it is always *now*. I must constantly bear this fact in mind. My emotional/ spiritual now contains neither my past nor my future. Consequently, my emotional past is dead and my future never arrives. When I confuse my emotional/spiritual world with the material/technological world, and attempt to manipulate emotional change, I find it thoroughly futile.

In the time-oriented material world, change *can* be made to happen. But since time does not exist in my emotional/spiritual world, I believe that emotional change must be allowed to *happen on its own,* without effort on my part. This distinction is very important to me.

Many of us in AA labor under the delusion that we can change our emotions on command, just as we can change happenings in the material/technological world. This is impossible for me because of the nonexistence of time in my emotional/spiritual world. When I accept my emotions each instant and do not attempt to change them, I find that emotional/spiritual changes automatically occur. Out of acceptance comes surrender. Out of surrender comes the willingness and openness for change.

▲ ▲ ▲ ▲ ▲

We have been taught that emotional troubles can be altered and reformulated at will by thinking. I believe that, instead, thought restricts emotional change. Thinking in the material, physical world *is* a valuable asset. However, in the emotional world, thinking can be a handicap.

I see all ideas and thought as occurring in the past. For example, the idea of the former sentence entered my mind, was transferred first to a portion of my brain that regulates muscle activity, and then my hand jotted it down. In the time it took this to occur, the idea became a microsecond of my past. Once I became aware that my past thoughts cannot solve my present emotional problems, my mind became quiet.

As an AA member, when I decided that my current *emotional* life cannot be changed by *thinking*, it dawned on me that a Power greater than myself can and will bring about the change. I ceased attempting to steer my emotional life and allowed the Second and Third Steps of AA to dawn on me and to function at will.

I learned—slowly, tediously, and with great turmoil—that I cannot change my emotional life any more than I can change the fact that I am addicted to alcohol and other drugs. The only thing that brings about change in me is a clear, uncritical awareness of my present emotional state and my allowing change to occur at its own natural pace spontaneously (just as my sobriety followed a clear, uncritical awareness of my addiction).

And yet, obviously and paradoxically, thinking and speaking are a part of my everyday life. I don't neglect them; I simply accept their restrictions and rely on the Second and Third Steps of AA to get me out of any emotional pickle.

THE GLORY OF THE TWELFTH STEP

As we share our experience, strength, and hope with everyone in our daily lives, intimacy develops. This in itself is healing. Emotional healing certainly occurs, and sometimes physical healing as well. Though we physicians may understand the anatomy of healing, we do not yet understand the essential *cause* of healing. That must be left to Powers much greater than us, on whom in good conscience we simply depend. Our own personal openness and our willingness to listen and to change constitute vital factors in expanding love, compassion, and healing in this universe. I believe that the following experience I had in Saigon relates to practicing the AA principles in "all my affairs."

I love to explore strange cities on foot, particularly in a country where I don't understand the language or customs and where I must rely on the resources of the universe to steer me back to my home base. There was a temple of worship in Saigon, named for a famous second-century Vietnamese warrior, whose spirit was said to protect it still. Usually only Vietnamese entered the sacred area.

One day I went into that temple. Statues of Buddha were distributed here and there—the fat Buddha, the thin Buddha, the starving Buddha, the ascetic Buddha, the weeping Buddha, the happy Buddha, and so forth. A magnificent red and gold altar stood at one wall. I caught the aroma of sweet incense. Everyone who came to meditate was expected to light a piece of incense, reminiscent of lighting candles in a Catholic church.

About thirty Vietnamese sat before the altar, meditating. Bells rang softly throughout the temple. All Far Eastern religions provide bells to bring people's wandering attention to the *now,* as Buddhists and Hindus revere the present minute. In the same way, some AA meetings open with a moment of silence or the Serenity Prayer, which brings members to the present moment.

I lighted an incense piece, placed it in the sand in a gold box beside the altar, sat, and meditated for a short time. I then left the temple. About fifty Vietnamese, wearing cloaks of various colors, were selling their wares in the vast courtyard: palmistry, ancestor worship books, the Tao, Tarot cards, magical healing services, and the like.

In a far corner of the square sat a Vietnamese man, meagerly dressed, with a black cloth spread before him. I asked him in broken Vietnamese if he would read my palm. When he agreed, I sat before him. My Vietnamese was poor at best, and his Montagnard dialect was totally unfamiliar to me, so a man standing nearby sized up the situation and interpreted in traditional Vietnamese. My palm reading was uneventful—not unlike palm readings I've had in the United States—although performed with ceremony and great aplomb.

When he finished, I caught a look of wonder in his eye. For some strange reason, we looked intently but warmly at one another for about five minutes. That is a long time! In his eyes I saw a variety of slowly changing moods: eagerness flowed into anxiety, then to tension, to anger, to hostility, to fear, and finally to a strange sort of childlike friendliness. Suddenly his eyes were vividly bright and I sensed that he had seen something mystical. Perhaps he thought that he was having contact with a true Buddha instead of a wayward USAID gynecologist. We continued to gaze at one another without blinking. A small crowd gathered around us. I was the only Caucasian in the area, but happily I was not apprehensive, and in fact felt calm and secure. After all, I wasn't harming him; I was simply looking into his eyes.

Still surrounded by the crowd, our eyes glued to each other, he slowly moved his hands to my face and gently touched my cheeks. I have no idea what possessed me, but I kissed his hands.

He did not resist, but continued to gaze at me, appearing overwhelmed and amazed. Our eyes were still locked as I slowly rose, walked backward to the temple gate, opened it, waved, and left.

For days I wondered what had happened. Why did we stare so intently at each other? What had created the openness in us? Why had I acted as I had? Why had he? I failed to find any answers, except that I had been both a participant and an observer at the same time—as I always tend to be. I cannot describe my inner feelings. But I asked myself more questions: if we honestly offer ourselves to another human being and make ourselves vulnerable, is it possible to connect deeply with him or her? Is this how success in AA Twelfth Step work comes about? Do we bring the magic of ourselves to a new AA member by telling our stories simply and poignantly—and through this process, do we transfer physical sobriety from one person to another? Or is this all magical nonsense?

I don't know and I suspect I never will. But the older I grow, the more I find that if I offer myself to those around me, and they to me, we not only seem to heal one another, but we also feel closer to one another, and our lives become more meaningful. I try to offer honest Twelfth Step work in all of my affairs.

But what does "practicing these principles in all our affairs" in the Twelfth Step of Alcoholics Anonymous *really* mean? How do we do this, and what do we accomplish by it?

To me, it means *quickly reviewing the first eleven AA Steps,* in order to determine whether or not an action is appropriate. A very rapid rundown reveals that:

▲ we need to recognize that we are powerless over controlling life—that if we try to do so, we find life quite unmanageable;

▲ we need power from another source for help;

▲ we need to take a quick inventory of our actions;

▲ we may need to talk—even briefly—with someone else, or with ourselves;

▲ we need to be truly willing and ready to allow the mystical powers of the universe to remove obstacles;

▲ we need to emit a deep human cry for help, and to be ready to perform any necessary legwork;

▲ we need to make amends, if required, and to take a moment-to-moment inventory of ourselves whenever speaking or acting;

▲ we need to rectify mistakes immediately and to realize that we do not run our own lives—it only seems as if we do.

Now, in a few seconds, that is a whole lot to ask. But that's what the Twelve Steps suggest: "practice these principles in *all* our affairs." So you see, for me, the glory of life is that basically life is the Twelfth Step in its broadest sense.

GOOD-BYE, SAIGON

In the fall of 1974 it seemed apparent that peace between North and South Vietnam would not last. The North Vietnamese army was heading towards the Mekong River Delta and the fertile rice fields, deep in South Vietnamese territory. I told my Vietnamese colleagues that I must return to the United States.

Ba Phep, my housekeeper, and Ba Soung, my driver, were deeply disturbed that I had to leave. So was I. Yet they understood. I gave Ba Phep enough money to set up a small sidewalk business, which she yearned to have. And to Ba Soung, who longed to return to farming, I gave sufficient funds to buy a small plot of land in her native area. Our parting was emotional. I hugged them both and wished them well in Vietnamese. Ba Soung drove me to the Saigon airport, and although she was a tough, wise, middle-aged woman who had made her way by her wits, we both broke out in tears. I told her in Vietnamese that she was wonderful and I would miss her. She very quietly said, "Chou Ohm," which means "Good-bye, sir." I walked through the gate, never to see her again.

Saigon had become my home. I left with a deep ache in my heart, but carrying glorious memories which are still with me today. Despite the intense heat, I could have lived there for the rest of my life. Of course, I was there on American economy—I doubt I would have been so content living on the far more stringent Vietnamese economy.

Our Vietnamese AA group had about seventeen members—sixteen Americans and one Vietnamese. We met in a Catholic church with the usual coffee, but also a basket of beautiful local fruit for snacking (the Vietnamese don't eat cookies). Mr. D., our Vietnamese member, was a scholar who had been addicted to opium and alcohol. He translated the *Twelve Steps and Twelve Traditions* into Vietnamese, but unfortunately there were too few native alcoholics for AA World Services to warrant publishing his translation. We held a small farewell party, as all the Americans were leaving Vietnam. Mr. D. stood in the church doorway that night and watched us all depart. I have never heard from him. I hope that he is still sober.

I flew to Singapore to spend several weeks at the KK hospital performing surgery and surgical sterilization in both men and women. The island is too small for a population increase, so the government encourages family planning, including sterilization and abortion. I loved Singapore, especially the Chinese section, which reminded me of Saigon.

I stayed at the Raffles Hotel; its bar is a legendary hangout for many famous writers and politicians. I, however, went to several AA meetings at a Singapore YMCA. Not one Oriental came to a meeting when I was there, but Caucasians from all over the world attended: merchant marines, engineers, and others in the city on temporary duty as I was. A colorful bunch—true rebels. Those AA meetings number among the best I've ever attended.

Sobriety and serenity

▲ ▲ ▲ ▲ ▲ ▲ ▲ ▲ ▲

"You are asking yourself, as all of us must: 'Who am I?' . . . 'Where am I?' . . . 'Whence do I go?' The process of enlightenment is usually slow. But, in the end, our seeking always brings a finding. These great mysteries are, after all, enshrined in complete simplicity."

Bill W., 1955 letter in
Came To Believe

Many AA members believe that a point will come when their lives are untroubled and serene. They equate length of sobriety with serenity, but in my opinion this is not necessarily true.

My serenity and insights grew rapidly after I traveled around the world in the late 1960s and early 1970s. And particularly after I discerned that it was the *search* for serenity which had kept serenity beyond my reach: my active search had implied that I could find serenity in the future. An utter impossibility!

For there was a fly in the ointment: I decided that *emotionally* there is no future . . . that emo-

tionally the time *is always now.* Once that became clear to me, my life became easier. I expended less effort in living and, indeed, felt more serene.

However, many years elapsed before I could claim that my judgment and foresight were solid. No matter how long I stay sober, my emotional growth never stops. Turmoil inevitably precedes expanding awareness. Even well into my Insight Period, though I felt better emotionally, I was still inclined to make errors and rather poor deductions. Today I still have my troubles, turmoils, and emotional pain, and I've been sober for a long time!

If it's true that in prolonged sobriety we are destined to arrive and remain at a pinnacle of quietness, wisdom, peace, and tranquility, then I have missed the boat. I wish I could say that I never have resentments—but I cannot. I wish I understood the nature of happiness—but I do not. I wish I always understood the intricacies of human relationships—but I do not. I wish I were able to advise younger AA members about how to avoid turmoil and trouble—but I cannot.

However, I *have* discovered that by following the AA Program as I have come to know it, a modicum of warmth and insight develops. I *have* learned that when I am in emotional trouble, I have failed to remember that the main point in life is *to live it—second by second*. Each of us is okay just the way we are at any given moment, irrespective of troubles and turmoils. We need these uncomfortable ingredients in order to grow and to expand our awareness. Pain and troubles have never worried me; in fact, I now welcome them, for they are forerunners of invaluable insight. *I see no emotional goal in life except to live it to its fullest—now! Pain or no pain!*

STEPS RETRACED—INDIA
TO SAN FRANCISCO

During my years in Southeast Asia, I was essentially a single man, although I did have a few romantic interludes.

The pending divorce between me and my second wife, Katie, had never been finalized. Katie had always fascinated me. We admired each other deeply, but we fought like bulldogs when we were together. This was agony, to be sure, but I must admit that it was exciting.

I had made a good number of trips through Southeast Asia when I lived in Saigon. Now I wanted to retrace my steps—particularly in India—en route back to the United States. I knew that Katie had long yearned to visit India: she was interested in Sri Easwaran and his followers at the Blue Mountain Center of Meditation, Tamales Bay, California. She wanted to make a pilgrimage to her guru's birthplace in the Blue Mountains of southern India. We decided to travel together.

By a stroke of luck, in the Blue Mountains of southern India we met a local farmer who had known Sri Easwaran. The farmer led us on foot to Easwaran's tiny hut. Tentatively, we entered through the unlocked front door. No one had lived there for a long, long time. The house was disheveled and covered with cobwebs, but an aura of ancient charm hovered over the place. We found two pictures on the mantel: one of a young woman who might have been Easwaran's first wife, the other of Easwaran in dinner clothes, seated with faculty from the university where he had taught English. Katie excitedly decided to take the two pictures with her and give them to Easwaran back in California. She seemed in a reverie, which I understood. This visit offered her a sense of completion about her guru, who meant so much to her. I thought I saw tears, but since she was not a crying sort, her tears must have been ones of devotion to Easwaran. We thanked our guide when we left the little house and continued our trip from the mountains to the plains of southern India.

During our trip, Katie and I talked of rekindling our marriage. Neither of us knew for sure that this was a good idea. Had I been wiser or my judgment sounder, I would have recognized the impracticality of our decision to try again. But in early 1975 we arrived in San Francisco. Impulsively—and perhaps it was a mistake—I agreed to return to the Bay Area and the University of California Medical School.

My beautiful five years in Southeast Asia were intimately tied to the Medical College of Georgia, which I now considered my professional home. I had previously spent many years at the University of California in San Francisco (UCSF), but the gynecological staff was new since my time. At Georgia I had been professor of obstetrics and gynecology. Now the UCSF Medical School offered me an appointment as *associate* professor. This galled me and I should have refused. But I accepted because I liked San Francisco, and I hoped that Katie and I might make it together.

The department chairman and his staff were very gracious to me. They were highly skilled, devoted to their work, enthusiastic, and creative. However, I had not realized that my foreign experiences had materially altered my medical point of view. I had grown accustomed to caring for the poor and needy, and to practicing medicine under very primitive conditions. The beautiful University of California and its innovative staff were just too much! I was professionally unhappy.

While I was overseas, Katie had built a small cottage in Bolinas, near San Francisco, and she wanted to remain there alone. I thought this a rather strange arrangement for a married couple trying to get back together again, but I stuck to my commitment to her. For two months I rented a room from friends in a Sausalito apartment, then I moved into a small apartment in San Francisco.

With the exception of the Forum, which was now my home group, I felt strange at AA meetings. I missed AA in Saigon. In my view, AA in California had changed.

Meanwhile, tensions once again built between Katie and me. We both realized that our relationship was untenable, and Katie finalized our divorce.

I resigned from UCSF. I realized that returning to San Francisco had been a poor decision, and I asked myself many questions: Why did I leave the Medical College of Georgia for UCSF Medical School? I had become friendly with faculty in Georgia, but felt unhappy and strange at UCSF. What possessed me to try to reinstate my marriage with Katie, when we'd had so many troubles in the past? I had somehow sensed that it would not work. When I resigned from UCSF, why didn't I return to the Medical College of Georgia? I could have, but I felt foolish and guilty because I had left only a few months before, and now my decision to return to California had blown up in my face.

Despite a rash of poor decisions, my insights had expanded and were increasing in depth and meaning. For example, my travels had given me a new view of people and their problems. In spite of recent turmoils with Katie, the University of California, and the Medical College of Georgia, I noted a sense of sweetness entering my life. The world seemed a better place. Though I was to experience more struggles, an inner mellowness and contentment had grown within me. I felt peaceful for long periods—days, weeks, even months—albeit my actions were still intense. But then, I had always been intense and acted impetuously.

Controversies in Kentucky

As I contemplated my next professional move just prior to resigning from UCSF, the president of the Appalachian Regional Hospitals in Lexington, Kentucky, telephoned with an invitation to consider developing a new department of obstetrics and gynecology at a hospital in Hazard, Kentucky. He referred me to Greg Cully, M.D., a board certified pediatrician, to discuss the matter, and I flew to Kentucky.

Hazard, in southeast Kentucky, is in a very rough coal mining area. (It's the home of the Hatfields and the McCoys!) Many inhabitants are poor, underprivileged, and need medical care desperately. My visit excited me. Hazard reminded me of Saigon—large numbers of people in need of good medical care—and that fact clinched it. I accepted the offer to locate there.

In September 1975 I pulled up stakes in San Francisco and moved to Hazard. The day I left California, I re-experienced the sense of freedom that I'd known five years before when I left all my possessions in Sausalito and went to Southeast Asia via Georgia. My trip to Kentucky was delightful and invigorating and I arrived, eager and enthusiastic. But unbeknownst to me and through no fault of mine, professional troubles awaited me.

Prior to my arrival, I'd held extensive telephone conversations with Dr. Greg Cully and with Russell Sword, administrator of the Hazard Appalachian Regional Hospital. Russell Sword had been cooperative about devising plans for my new obstetrics and gynecology clinic, which was to be on the first floor of the hospital. When I arrived in Hazard, construction was only half finished, but the clinic would be ready for patients within two months. Meanwhile, I'd been asked to offer gynecological and obstetrical consultations when needed, and I readily agreed.

The monthly hospital staff meeting was scheduled for the evening I arrived. The medical staff was not large—approximately twenty. I sensed tension. Two doctors were especially cool: Drs. X and Y. When the chief of staff introduced me, I explained that I'd be happy to perform gynecological surgery and would be available for obstetrical complications. I expressed my delight at having three excellent midwives available to perform routine deliveries. My remarks were greeted with polite applause.

"New business" was announced. Dr. X quickly moved that the midwives—hired for me by Dr. Cully—not be allowed to deliver babies unless I was present. Swiftly, his motion was seconded and passed.

I was shocked. One condition for my coming was that I not be on call for routine obstetrics, but only for obstetrical complications. I could see that I represented competition for Dr. X. Despite being angered beyond belief, I held myself in control. But before I could defend the midwives, the chief of staff adjourned the meeting. Within moments Dr. Cully and I were alone in the room.

Dr. Cully was rabid about Dr. X's maneuver. I told him that I'd better return to California, but he urged me to stay. Had my judgment been intact prior to leaving California, I would have insisted on an agreement in writing about my hospital activities in Hazard, a description of the midwives' duties, and my connection with them. But I had not done this. I'd moved to Hazard impulsively, after one brief visit and a few telephone conversations with Dr. Cully and the president of the Appalachian Regional Hospitals. Long-term sobriety had hardly sharpened my judgment in this case! Nevertheless, I agreed to remain in Hazard.

This rocky beginning colored my entire tenure at the Hazard Appalachian Regional Hospital. I was irritable, tense, nervous, resistant, and I refused to monitor the midwives during deliveries. Drs. X and Y objected strenuously. In retaliation, I referred all obstetrical patients to other physicians in the community. But the fate of my midwives was in jeopardy, so I obtained permission from the hospital administrator to use them as nurses in my clinic. They *were* highly skilled nurses, and a great asset to me. But they did not practice midwifery in the Appalachian Regional Hospital! Though Drs. X, Y, and I eventually respected one another, we were never especially friendly.

On the whole, however, I enjoyed my stay in Hazard. My gynecological work was enjoyable and productive, and I made friends among other doctors, nurses, and my patients. However, I was never completely trusted by anyone in the area. Inhabitants of the southeastern Kentucky mountains do not trust "outsiders," and I was no exception.

LOVELY FREDA
AND KENTUCKY AA

"Everyone should be married three times."
Margaret Mead, lecture in 1940s at Chestnut Lodge Sanitarium,
Rockville, Maryland

One day I met a delightful and friendly young woman named
Freda in a Hazard restaurant. I was struck by her intense beauty and
her quick repartee. We bantered back and forth and flirted for a
few minutes. For days, I could not get Freda off my mind. So about
three weeks later I called her, and we had dinner and went for a
drive. Even though I was thirty years older than Freda, we became
enmeshed in a whirlwind romance.

Freda's husband had died a few months before we met, leaving
some insurance to help in the care of their two boys. She had
attended nursing school for one year before marrying, and wanted
to return. Her marriage had been a troubled one and the tragic
death of her husband left its scar. But Freda was resilient, and she
handled her troubles masterfully. I could not help but admire her.

Freda was sad following her husband's death, and I was sad
following my two divorces. Each of us was pleased to have found
the other. After six months, in spite of great misgivings and a good
number of inner warning signals on my part, Freda and I were
married. Many Hazard residents were surprised and disapproving.
Our disparate ages was one concern, and the length of Freda's
widowhood was another. Her husband had been dead for only
seven months, and in Kentucky, a "good woman" does not remarry
until her husband has been gone for at least a year. I found our

marriage quite satisfactory, even though Freda attended the University of Kentucky Nursing School 125 miles away in Lexington. She had her boys with her, and we were together only on weekends.

Through Freda and her family, I put to rest some ghosts concerning my Nebraska background. I'd been born in Omaha and lived there until age eleven. I despised that fact. I had miserable memories of being poor and, I thought, underprivileged. I believed that I'd been born on the wrong side of the tracks. Two uncles on my mother's side were rather well-to-do physicians, and I felt that my family was the poor branch of the family tree. In a sense, I suppose, it was. We frequently received hand-me-down clothing from the relatives, which were given in a warm and friendly manner. But I didn't know this, and thought that the clothing made us the low members of a highbrow family. For many years I harbored these untrue and exaggerated images of my family's status.

Compared with Freda's family, my family's scale of living in Omaha was more than adequate. Freda and her six brothers were raised in a typical two-room coal miner's house in Hazard. Freda's father, a miner, had died of "black lung." Freda's mother, Granny, was remarkably staunch, stalwart, deeply religious, and a true survivor. She had raised her children to be the same. Her daughter, her sons and their wives, and her grandchildren all considered Granny's small house the family's congregation center. Though the house was cramped, they seemed happy together. I was three years older than Granny, but we had a beautiful relationship; she referred to me as "one of my young'uns." Freda, the boys, and I lived across the street from Granny.

This wonderful family helped me to re-evaluate my memories of Omaha. I began to appreciate the material things we'd had in my youth, but I wished that my brother and I had been as close to our parents as Granny was to her family. Of course, my parents were alcoholic; Freda's were not. Joining Granny's family, learning to love and admire them all, improved my capacity to develop closeness with other people, and thereby also improved the quality of my sobriety.

Some members of Alcoholics Anonymous tend to think that the major way to change emotionally is to simply attend AA meetings and read AA literature. To a great degree this is correct. But involvement in our local communities can also aid our sober growth. I loved my involvement with Freda and her family. When I later returned to Omaha and drove by my boyhood home, I felt a glow of inner warmth, rather than a dull, despondent ache. What a relief!

I could find no evidence of AA in Hazard. The AA General Service Office in New York knew of no group in my immediate area. There were a few AA meetings in Lexington, but that was 125 miles away. So for a year, I only attended meetings during an occasional trip to Lexington. I might not recommend this sort of relocation to newer AA members, but I had been sober for twenty-three years when I moved to Hazard.

After about a year, Beth—a GSO secretary—phoned to say that there *was* an AA member in Hazard: an attorney named Joe C. Delighted, I called on him.

Joe C. was well known in Hazard. Typically for that community, he was rather suspicious of outsiders. He was especially suspicious of me, as an enthusiastic, overly verbal Californian. Joe was a tight-lipped, taciturn Kentuckian. We simply did not hit it off. However, he told me that there was another AA member in town—a woman—and that the two of them met on Monday evenings in Joe's office.

Now the AA membership in Hazard increased to three. Unhappily the lady died shortly after that, and our "group" returned to a membership of two. Though Joe and I did not see eye to eye on many things, we *were* sober, and we met every Monday night in his office . . . a sort of unhappy AA duo! My wife, Freda, read the Big Book, liked the purpose of AA, and wanted to join Joe's group. But that was a closed meeting (for alcoholics only) and Freda was not alcoholic. Consequently, I started a Tuesday night open meeting at the Appalachian Regional Hospital, and published a notice in the local newspaper. Freda and I gathered two or three newcomers. One was Pappy, a house painter and a great guy who became a close friend of mine. Another was Perry G., six foot four, 220 pounds, an imposing man with a deep, booming voice. I learned to love Perry very much, and though he had trouble staying sober, he was a source of much amusement and fun for us.

From an AA standpoint, my time in Hazard was trying. No one in the hospital group maintained sobriety except Pappy and me. I missed the California AA groups. But I kept in touch with the Program through the two small meetings in Hazard, and by corresponding with the New York GSO office and with friends in California and elsewhere. I was a longtime subscriber to the *AA Grapevine,* which I read each month from cover to cover. I contributed a couple of articles to the *Grapevine* while I lived in Hazard.

During my second year in Kentucky, travel increased my AA meetings. Freda and I went to Europe, South America, and California, attending meetings in all. In South America (this was the mid-1970s) I could find only Spanish-speaking groups.

MY PALM SPRINGS AA DISASTER

"To my mind, one of the most significant sentences in the entire book Alcoholics Anonymous *is this: 'Some of us have tried to hold on to our old ideas and the result was nil until we let go absolutely.' The rigidity with which even some non-drinking alcoholics will cling to the opinions, beliefs, and convictions they had upon entering AA is well-nigh incredible. One of the major objectives of AA therapy is to help the alcoholic finally recognize these ideas and become willing to relinquish his death grip on them."*

A Member's Eye View of Alcoholics Anonymous

In 1978 I decided to retire from the Appalachian Regional Hospital. I was dissatisfied with my medical arrangements in Hazard. I got along well with most of the local physicians—but not all. And since my Saigon days, I had developed hot feet. As I examined my last patient during my final day in my Hazard office, Chuck C. telephoned from Laguna Beach, California. Chuck C. was the AA member I'd admired when I was newly sober.

Chuck and I had drifted apart over the years, and had even had a few unfriendly encounters. However, Chuck had read some *Grapevine* articles I'd written, and he'd figured that I'd changed. He invited me to give a talk at the Palm Springs (California) Round-up. (I had given my Blackboard Talk at this Round-up about a dozen years before.) I was pleased to hear from Chuck C., for I really loved him very much.

The audience had anticipated an AA speaker who would entertain them. Instead I delivered a rather serious talk. I described my trials and tribulations during twenty-five years of sobriety. I explained that the majority of those painful events had been sorted out, had faded, and that I now felt at peace with myself.

Apparently my presentation was inappropriate for that banquet. It fell flat and I was terribly chagrined. My talk was later criticized by many Round-up members. Once again I became aware of a contingent in AA whom I have tagged the "I am right" or "I know the way" boys.

After the Palm Springs Round-up fiasco, I put my AA tail between my legs and scooted back to Kentucky. In spite of prolonged sobriety, I had not quite learned to go my own way with confidence, irrespective of others' expectations. I have since learned that we must each respect our own way in AA and, when criticized, let the chips fall where they may—that waiting for someone else's approval is a sheer waste of time. I cannot validate myself through others.

Back in Hazard, I felt lost because I had retired from the hospital and really had nothing to do. I was not accustomed to a relaxed, easy, armchair type of life. But after decades of fighting, jostling, and jousting in travail, I welcomed an interval of professional inactivity—albeit a short one.

The 'I know the way' boys

▲ ▲ ▲ ▲ ▲ ▲ ▲ ▲ ▲

The "I know the way" or "I am right" boys are AA members who, in my opinion, believe that only *they* know how the AA Program should be lived, and are critical of anyone who deviates from their traditional line. My inclination is to avoid them. Yet I know that if I, myself, become one of the "I know the way" boys, other people will avoid me too!

I felt uncomfortable with the "I am right" boys for years, but now I am at peace with these feelings. I have decided that they have a right to express themselves, even if I disagree with them, just as I have a right to express myself. Given the AA world as *they see it,* they cannot help but feel that they are correct. So, in fact, I have nothing to resent or to hate. An AA slogan covers this with deceptive simplicity: "Live and Let Live."

For me, there is *no* way; there is no *real* program of Alcoholics Anonymous. There is only *your* way and *my* way. In the Twelve Steps, the words "as we understood Him" define not only *your* concept of God, but also, in my opinion, *your* personal AA program. I discovered long ago that when I believe in my own personal program, I am then ready to allow others to believe in theirs.

During my Insight period, I saw that we in AA are all human beings staying sober together—as a unit. This does not mean that my resentments have ended, but rather that resentments, dislikes, and irritabilities represent signposts along the way of my growth. These never completely disappear —rather, because of them, growth occurs.

Perhaps the "I know the way" boys have not, as yet, experienced this.

A RESOUNDING 'YES' TO NEPAL

". . . Dr. Earle M . . . had also obtained Patrick's address through the Loners-Internationalists Service {A.A. members who cannot, for various reasons, attend meetings, write to one another by means of this service}. . . . His room is two doors from mine in the hotel. We are together two or three times a day. I find him extremely interesting and a great help to me, since he was such a close friend of Bill W., our co-founder. What an enriching experience, to hear so much about the history of AA from Dr. Earle, here in this strange place. For that I am grateful. . . ."

C.G.,"Scaling New Heights,"
AA Grapevine, March 1979

Shortly after my return from Palm Springs, William Oldham, M.D., of the Department of Population at USAID in Washington, D.C., telephoned. A urologist whom I'd known in Saigon, Dr. Oldham was now Director of Population Studies in Nepal. He needed a physician to work with him on a population study in Nepal with two objectives: patient education concerning fertility control, and teaching surgical sterilization techniques (in men and women) to the Nepali physicians. Would I like to spend several months with this family planning project in Nepal? A permanent assignment might later be offered.

I had no difficulty in saying a resounding "yes." Freda was agreeable that I go.

I attended a three-week course on population control (including surgical sterilization) at Johns Hopkins University in Baltimore. From there I went to Manila; USAID had arranged for me to spend five weeks with Virgilio Oblepias, M.D., an oncologist especially interested in surgical sterilization, from whom I learned a great deal.

Then I went on to Katmandu in Nepal. I stayed at the excellent small hotel Woodlands for the next four months.

GSO in New York had given me the name of a recovering alcoholic Catholic priest in Katmandu. Father Patrick G. was a Maryknoll Father who had lived in Asia for many years. He had joined AA in the Philippine Islands fifteen years before I met him. In Katmandu, he had been an "AA loner"—the only AA member in Nepal—corresponding with the Loners-Internationalists secretary at GSO, until Jack B. of Springfield, Virginia, went to work at the airport in Katmandu.

About four months later, Claude G. of La Salle, Quebec, an aerial map photographer sober only a few months, moved to Katmandu. I arrived shortly after that.

The first evening that Patrick, Jack, Claude, and I had an AA meeting at Father G.'s place, we also held a business meeting. There we founded the Mt. Everest Group of AA in Katmandu. We met twice a week, and by the time I left Nepal, we'd collected three or four more members, all Nepali. They didn't really understand AA, but even if they didn't stay sober, at least they cut down on their drinking. I understand from Father G. that the Mt. Everest group has grown very large, and today includes several sober Nepali members. Claude was so entranced by the founding of the Mt. Everest AA meeting that he wrote an article about it for the *Grapevine*.

The meeting of the four of us AA members in Nepal is an example of how it can be a small world in the AA Program. No matter where you go, AA is there. If it isn't, you can organize a meeting.

I loved Nepal, especially Katmandu. The weather was much like San Francisco, and Dr. Oldham and I worked well together. During my four months there, work was frequently interrupted by Nepali holidays, which provided opportunities to explore the cities of Katmandu, Pokhara, Lumbini (Buddha's birthplace), and other villages.

At the end of three months I was asked if I wanted a long-term tour of duty. I'd fallen in love with Katmandu but said that I must first consult my family in Hazard, Kentucky. When I mentioned that my stepsons were still in school, the director of the Population Studies offered to send the two boys, who were ten and twelve, to a British school in southern India, which sounded very exciting to me. I wrote Freda about this unique offer. Freda rejected it by return mail; neither she nor the boys could bring themselves to leave Kentucky. I was deeply disappointed and returned to the United States feeling defeated.

My family's refusal to leave Kentucky on any durable basis made me feel imprisoned. I liked Hazard and our marriage, but I'd enjoyed too many worldwide experiences to be comfortable long-term in a small Kentucky town. I said nothing, but this was the turning point in our marriage. We were to divorce one year later.

I Found a Compatriot

"Physiology, not psychology, determines whether one drinker will become addicted to alcohol and another will not."

Dr. James R. Milam and **Katherine Ketcham**, *Under the Influence*

On my return from Nepal in 1978 I obtained a position as staff gynecologist in a family planning clinic called Surgical Arts in Louisville, Kentucky. Since I worked there several days a week, I maintained an apartment in Louisville, although my actual home was still in Hazard.

My evenings in Louisville were free, so I attended many AA meetings. There was the Token Club, an Alano Club of sorts (Alano Clubs are free-standing club houses, run by AA members but not officially connected with Alcoholics Anonymous. Alano Clubs are found predominantly in the West). Members of the Token Club in Louisville were devoted, while also easy and free-wheeling. Meetings were held frequently throughout the day.

I met a first-class example of a loving, helping member of AA in Louisville. Jack S. was a former railroad man, and his life was devoted tirelessly to helping alcoholic railroad men. I enjoyed simply observing his AA devotion. Jack was a great friend, and we attended many meetings together.

After several months in Louisville I met Dr. W., a recovering alcoholic physician. He worked at the Surgical Arts Clinic and was a professor at the University of Louisville Medical School. Dr. W. arranged an appointment at the medical school in 1979 for me to lecture to the medical students on human sexuality.

Dr. W. visited the Payne Whitney Alcoholic Rehabilitation Center in Baltimore and brought back a monograph written by James R. Milam, Ph.D., *The Emergent Comprehensive Concept of Alcoholism* (now out of print). By now I had been presenting my Blackboard Talk on the physical aspects of alcoholism and recovery for many years. Dr. Milam's monograph was a mirror of my Blackboard Talk—but far more comprehensive. At last I had found a compatriot!

Dr. Milam lived in Kirkland, Washington. When I telephoned him from Louisville, his response was warm and friendly. I told him my name and that I was a gynecologist and a member of AA. I started to explain why I thought his monograph was wonderful, but before I could utter another word, he said, "Wait a minute. Aren't you Dr. Earle?"

Surprised, I said, "Yes. Dr. Earle is how AA people usually refer to me."

Dr. Milam continued quickly. "Let me tell you a story." He said that through some AA members in 1966 he'd heard a tape of my Blackboard Talk. He'd liked it very much and told me that it had been a stimulating factor in his further research into the biological/genetic aspects of alcoholism, which led eventually to writing his monograph.

I was dumbfounded. I asked Dr. Milam if Dr. W. and I could travel to Kirkland to see him. He readily agreed.

In the fall of 1979, both Dr. W. and I traveled to Kirkland and observed Dr. Milam's principles at work in Alcenas Hospital.

Meanwhile, Dr. Milam and writer Katherine Ketcham were collaborating on their book *Under the Influence,* which clarified his original concept in lay language. That book is a gem. Every recovering alcoholic should read it, and then re-read it. Dr. W. and I were excited and impressed by our week in Kirkland. I felt a strong urge to move to Kirkland for further observations of Dr. Milam's work. There was even talk of my possibly assuming an interim medical directorship at Alcenas Hospital.

Back in Hazard, when I told Freda that I wanted to move all of us to Kirkland, I found great resistance. It became very clear to me then that they were too deeply entrenched to *ever* leave Kentucky. We agreed that I would go to Kirkland alone.

I'll never forget the day I left Hazard. The boys were at school, and Freda was at work. I was alone in the house. As I stood in the living room, I felt lost, lonely, and somewhat depressed—yet at the same time eager and excited by my plan to work with Dr. Milam. I departed without fanfare, sensing that I would never return—and I never did. Several months later, Freda and I realized that we should divorce. And we did.

I do have some regrets about the ending of that marriage. I spent a good number of days feeling that I loved Freda, but aware that the thirty-year age difference between us was an important factor. I still talk to her on the phone a couple of times a year; she and the boys are fine.

GETTING HELP, GIVING HELP

"Practically every AA member declares that no satisfaction has been deeper and no joy greater than in a Twelfth Step job well done."

Twelve Steps and Twelve Traditions

I drove the southern route from Kentucky to the state of Washington, stopping several times to attend AA meetings. When I arrived in Flagstaff, Arizona, I contacted the local AA office. A member came to my hotel that evening and took me to a meeting. About fifteen young men were there—all sober less than six months. But they were eager and attentive. I explained that I'd been driving for several days and was fatigued and drained.

They addressed many remarks to me and were very nurturing. I felt revived at the end of the meeting.

Sometimes length of sobriety means far less than the quality of sobriety. Although I'd been sober for many years (I didn't tell the young men how long) and I knew a great deal about AA, the Flagstaff group of fifteen relative newcomers had effectively rejuvenated me. That's the magic of AA.

Refreshed, I left the next day for San Francisco, where I spent a few days with old AA friends, attended meetings, and even did a little Twelfth Step work. An old friend with long-term sobriety had lost his wife. He was desperate and ready to drink. I called him. We had dinner together, and he—like me in Flagstaff—seemed refreshed. And so it goes: we pass the message on.

Listening as a form of surrender

▲ ▲ ▲ ▲ ▲ ▲ ▲ ▲ ▲

"Surrender" is a common word in Alcoholics Anonymous. Surrender of the ego, a spiritual maneuver, is integral to the framework of sobriety. But just *how* we surrender emotionally and spiritually can be perplexing.

I learned something of surrender in Saigon, when I realized that my *search* for serenity had been my trouble. To search for something implies that it can be found in the future. But I believe that *there is no future,* emotionally and spiritually speaking. Instead, I *accept what is* with no demand that it be different. This allows emotional change to happen to me spontaneously.

Over the ensuing years I've learned more about surrender. I had played with the idea that listening to and learning from everybody and everything might not only constitute surrender, but could define humility.

I've realized that, for me, most interpersonal communication happens through body language and other nonverbal techniques. (What you *do* speaks to me so loudly that I can't hear what you *say*!) Words are really a minor fragment in communication. Listening to words is far more important than speaking them. I began to equate listening with surrender.

I believe that if I try to listen without condoning or condemning, simply in order to understand what is being said, I am in a state of surrender. For example: if I take my troubles to a friend, and he or she listens to me with only one idea in mind—*to understand what I am trying to say*—then he or she will neither agree nor disagree with my words.

All my life I yearned to meet someone who would simply *hear* me—not advise me, not criticize me, not even agree with me—just *hear* me. And my listening, nonjudgmental friend does just that. Being heard this way makes me eager to tell more. And my friend knows that through *really* listening, he or she will connect with me. So he or she listens to me with even more intensity.

And the two of us connect through the art of listening.

During the course of our conversation, we experience equivalent emotional intensity: our energies, attention, devotion, and interests can be equal. With our energies thus marshalled and pinpointed, listening to and understanding one another replaces our individual egos. Surrender occurs when egos are no longer in the way.

AA members know that ego surrender is vital for recovery from alcoholism and for the maintenance of sobriety. But I believe that there is no way to give up the ego voluntarily, for the very act of attempting to give it up was, for me, a form of hanging on. Yet *listening in order to understand* led me to *involuntary* surrender of the ego. This, to me, is one of the most important factors in the spiritual structure that underlies sobriety.

I see nonjudgmental listening as the epitomy of "sharing our experience, strength and hope" with one another in order to recover. It is at this point that healing begins to happen.

Coasting in Washington

I found a small apartment in Kirkland, in a complex with a pool, exercise room, sauna, and spa. By the time I arrived, however, new owners and management had taken over Dr. Milam's hospital and my possible interim position did not materialize. So my stay in Kirkland was a vacation and long-needed rest.

In the northwestern United States, due to lots of rain and sunshine, everything seemed to be in blossom. Even the buildings seemed bright and new.

The aura surrounding Alcoholics Anonymous and its members felt just as new. Being with active AA was an enormous relief and stimulus to me. The enthusiasm for sobriety exhilarated me. AA meetings were held everywhere, at all times of day. Some people attended two or three meetings a day. Men's stag luncheon groups, known as the Union Clubs, met daily at various locations. I loved the Union Clubs—they reminded me of our Forum at Children's Hospital in San Francisco. Here, too, a topic would be chosen and discussions were lively.

The Hilltop Alano Club in Bellevue, Washington, was a beehive of AA activity. Meetings began at 5:30 A.M. and ended at 11:00 P.M. Each meeting attracted about fifty members. I made a good number of friends in Washington AA: Al F., Dr. Janice P., Jack and Laurie M., Art E., and others. I still keep in touch with most of them.

My short (five-month) stay in the Seattle-Bellevue-Kirkland area was relaxing as well as invigorating. I was no longer practicing obstetrics and gynecology nor doing professional counseling. I coasted, enjoying the time for repair and reflection. I had experienced many things in my many years of sobriety. I had trudged through the Irritable and Inventive Periods of my AA life, and was well into my Insight Period. I had always been infatuated with AA, but now my infatuation had taken a turn toward inner rest. I had no obligations. I had been married and divorced three times. I had traversed the globe seven times, and had spent several years in such disparate areas as Southeast Asia and Kentucky. My pace in the past had been fast, but in the Northwest, I finally began to slow down.

MEETING MICKEY—AND MARRIAGE

Wardell B. Pomeroy, Ph.D., a co-author of the Kinsey sex studies, had been academic dean of the Institute for Advanced Study of Human Sexuality in San Francisco since the mid-1970s. When I was in Kirkland in 1980, I phoned him to say hello, as I did from time to time. I mentioned an urge to return—yet again—to the San Francisco Bay Area. He asked if I would consider a position as medical director of the institute. Intrigued, I went to San Francisco to discuss the idea further.

Though I didn't know it, I was about to meet Mickey, my wife-to-be. We met under circumstances which were unusual, fun, and even comical.

Mickey was a Ph.D. candidate at the institute. She was accumulating data for her dissertation on the sexual behavior of alcoholic women. She needed another expert for her dissertation committee, one who was knowledgeable in the fields of both sexuality and alcoholism. Wardell Pomeroy suggested to Mickey that she invite me to join her committee.

When I arrived in San Francisco, Wardell and I had lunch, then we retired to the massage/hot tub room at the Institute. We removed our clothes, climbed into the redwood hot tub, and discussed old times as we soaked. Suddenly Wardell remembered Mickey. He phoned the upstairs office, where she worked part-time, and asked her to come down to meet me.

When Mickey arrived she took off her clothes, climbed into the hot tub, and Wardell formally introduced us! Vibrantly and vivaciously, Mickey explained her study to me, then asked me to join her dissertation committee.

I looked at this remarkable little ball of fire, grinned, and said, "I'll do better than that—I'll *marry* you!" I wasn't serious, of course, but little did I know that in time Mickey *would* become my wife!

We joked and bantered back and forth in the hot tub. I was attracted to this spirited woman, and as we left the room, I kissed her in a manner which implied: I'll see you again—later.

During that visit, I accepted the post as medical director of the Institute. Within two weeks I'd left Kirkland, moved back to San Francisco, and was settled in an apartment close to the institute. It was still my nature to move fast!

When I met Mickey, she was rebuilding her life after the dissolution of an eighteen-year marriage to an active alcoholic. He'd been hospitalized several times, and in and out of AA, but he couldn't stay sober for long. For many years he and Mickey had lived in the Bahamas, where they had established a successful temporary office help service. They also had lived in Jamaica, England, and France. Eventually alcohol tooks its toll on the marriage and on the Bahamas business. Mickey had been in Al-Anon since 1969, and she finally decided to throw in the towel, return to the United States, and file for divorce.

With little money, but eager and employable, she went from being vice president of her own Bahamas business for fourteen years, to being an accounts/payroll clerk for a small marketing firm in San Francisco. Slowly and surely, with the help of Al-Anon and personal counseling, she rehabilitated herself.

Mickey was determined to return to school and learn a new career. First she earned her B.A. from Antioch College/West. Next she was accepted in an advanced degree program at the Institute for Advanced Study of Human Sexuality. Because of long-term personal experience with alcoholism, she focused her Ph.D. research on the sexuality of alcoholic women. Her dissertation, *The Sexual Behavior of Alcoholic Women While Drinking and During Sobriety*, was to be completed in October 1982.

Mickey is a vibrant, open, honest, direct woman without pretense. She is nonthreatening, sexually on fire, lacks prejudice, and is tolerant about all aspects of life—including human sexuality. She moves fast, assumes enormous obligations, carries them out, and does not tire easily—but when she does, she collapses. She does not cry readily—but when she does, she floods. At times, like all of us, she hides her feelings—but not for long. Never have I seen a woman be so completely trusted by her friends and acquaintances. She is verbally quick, nimble on her feet, possesses keen insight into human strengths and failings, and speaks directly about them—but with tenderness. Her spontaneity is similar to mine; after all, we are both Leos.

I quickly learned to admire and love her, and my feelings have not waned. Rather they have grown. I feel fortunate to have married her and to share her life. And for both of us, it's about time!

We have each weathered more marriages and divorces than most people (seven between us). The struggle to arrive where we are has been a long one. I believe that it's a blessing we didn't meet earlier in our lives because we both had too much to process first. We were brought together at the appropriate time. Early in our romance, thinking that we had had our share of mates and partners, we promised one another that we would not marry. "We've had too many!" we agreed. This lasted for a year. Then one day, out of the blue, we followed our deepest wishes and planned the inevitable: marriage. Thank goodness we did.

After settling with Mickey in Oakland, I was eager to reunite with AA in the San Francisco Bay Area. I expected the AA groups to be the same as when I left many years before. But the old saying "You can't go home again" was true in this instance. Many of my old cronies were gone, and some were even dead. For a while I felt lost and ill at ease at meetings. After several months, however, I realized that the problem was mine.

San Francisco Bay Area AA had changed and expanded. For example, meetings now lasted an hour and a half. (In my early days, no alcoholic could sit longer than one hour!) Once I realized that the groups were not the same as when I left, I felt friendly toward San Francisco AA again. I could see that our Program would never be static, but would continually grow and change. Some members resent this, some love it, but change continues. I—for one—am glad.

Mickey had joined Al-Anon in England in 1969, and had also attended meetings in the Bahamas and the San Francisco Bay Area. So it seemed right and natural for us to attend AA and Al-Anon meetings together. We have lots of fun being "old-timers"—sometimes we relax together on the sidelines, *trying* not to appear too owlish and wise!

Returning to live in the San Francisco Bay Area felt like coming home. Integrating with the new AA scene brought a warm, friendly glow. By now I realized that everyone, whether in AA or not, needs other human beings. For years, I'd lived in isolation, in a world unique to me. Now I saw that I need other people for my life to be complete. This does not mean a dependence on anyone, nor that I expect others to live my life for me, nor that I am relieved of my personal responsibilities. But it does mean that my unique-ness needs to be combined with everyone else's uniqueness, so that a sense of harmony and continuity can develop.

By now I recognized that I am but one small part of the enormous fabric of life. I had long and secretly savored the idea that I could live without anyone. I had often felt resentful and suspi-cious. Now I saw this to be egocentric, self-centered, and really restricting. On my high and mighty throne of aloofness, I had felt that I didn't need others, so I avoided them. No longer! My world travels and long years in the AA Program convinced me that I genuinely need others in order to feel warm and alive.

Yes, I still require long intervals of silence and of being by myself. But no longer as maneuvers to eliminate others from my life. After a period of being alone, returning to the hubbub of life gives me a sense of continuity. To be in solitude and at the same time together with others essentially represents two ways of saying the same thing: we are individuals; we are all one! What a joy that discovery was!

In the early 1980s I reunited with Rich K., an old AA friend from the SYESH and Floorsitter days of the 1960s. Now sober and clean for many years, Rich had become an accomplished Oriental-style brush painter. We had fun talking about the old days. We hiked and ate vegetarian foods together. Rich was a chemical dependency counselor at the Merritt Peralta Institute (MPI), a chemical dependency treatment center, and fit into the MPI family very nicely. He and Mickey and I attended many AA meetings together. But after several years, Rich decided to return to his original home in Yucca Valley near Palm Springs. We miss him.

My stay at the Institute for Advanced Study of Human Sexuality lasted about a year. I enjoyed it and was grateful to have met Mickey there, but other professional involvements awaited both of us.

COUNSELING RECOVERING PROFESSIONALS

"Various support groups limited to professionals have developed parallel to and within AA. Most do not attempt to compete with or replace AA."

LeClair Bissell, M.D., and **Paul Haberman,**
Alcoholism in the Professions

In 1980 I started a private counseling practice for groups of recovering addicted professionals: physicians, dentists, pharmacists, an occasional nurse, veterinarians, some attorneys, some educators, and a smattering of high-level corporate executives. All were addicted to alcohol, a variety of drugs, or both. Because alcoholism/drug addiction is seen as a family disease, spouses and family members were urged to join the groups. This proved a marked asset for most; recovery is generally far more rewarding when experienced together.

My wife Mickey, an experienced group leader, was my co-director. For many months prior to that, Jody Yeary, Ph.D., had been my group co-leader. The professional groups met on "Pill Hill" in Oakland. Our treatment mode included education about addiction and cross-addiction, supportive group therapy, a rich flavoring of Alcoholics Anonymous tenets, and many of the principles about treating alcoholics/drug addicts that I had embraced thus far in my Insight Period.

These recovering professionals seemed to us to be characteristically self-propelled and markedly egocentric—an asset in their work, but they did not easily accept the AA Program. We gave everyone copies of the Big Book (*Alcoholics Anonymous*), AA's

Twelve Steps and Twelve Traditions, and a medical paper that we distributed on addiction (see p. 237). We frequently referred to AA's Steps and literature, and we encouraged attendance at AA, NA, Al-Anon, and NarAnon meetings. Each group had volunteers who introduced other members to AA and/or NA by taking them to meetings. Many continued to go—some did not.

Each group met three times a week. At one meeting, nonaddicted spouses and family members met separately with Mickey, while the addicted met with me.

We recommended James Milam's and Katherine Ketcham's book *Under the Influence.* We told our professional groups that in our opinion alcoholism/drug addiction is predominantly a biogenetic disease, and that susceptibility to it is inherited from one generation to the next. I gave segments of my Blackboard Talk to show the biological variations of both liver and brain metabolism in the alcoholic/drug addict. We emphasized our belief that *although individuals are not responsible for their addictive disease, they are very responsible for their own recoveries.*

We repeatedly underscored our conviction that prolonged toxicity lingers in recovery, especially in alcoholics. We encouraged open discussion about physical and emotional feelings, and reassured group members that a great deal of how they felt was due to toxicity from prolonged use of alcohol/drugs. This important point was difficult for some recovering individuals to accept and to remember. Recovering people whom I have known seem to easily assume the destructive attitudes which were laid on them by their families and others. They tend to be haunted by the traditional but inaccurate myths that their addiction is their fault, and the belief that they should have been able to use more will power. Such feelings, unless addressed and cleared, damage the development of sobriety.

We stressed the importance of proper nutrition. We urged members to read the book *Eating Right to Live Sober* by Katherine Ketcham and L. Ann Mueller, M.D., and to follow the diets in it. To prove our point, most group members went to dinner together after meetings with Mickey and me. Not only was this an excellent chance for them to learn to order foods that were, in our opinion, appropriate for recovery, but it also offered an opportunity to practice rebuilding socializing skills.

I believe that about 85 percent of alcoholics/drug addicts have varying degrees of hypoglycemia (abnormally low level of glucose in the blood) which may decline in some recovering alcoholics as time goes by. Hypoglycemics metabolize sugar abnormally. Symptoms of the "low blood sugar syndrome" in the alcoholic/drug addict can include: excessive hunger, tremulousness, sweating, depression, loss of self-esteem, irritability, a sense of feeling lost, abusiveness, and a tendency to lash out at those around them. Simple table sugar (or the hidden sugars in foods) can trigger this tragic roller coaster ride of painful physical and emotional symptoms. Consequently, we urged our groups to avoid sugar.

We taught that exercise is vital to recovery. In my opinion, biogenetically, alcoholics/drug addicts have naturally lower endorphin levels than do nonaddicts. Exercise temporarily increases the endorphin level, leading to the sort of "high" described by many joggers. We urged recovering people to exercise daily, because the endorphin high from exercise is transient.

On weekend mornings Mickey and I met the groups in Tilden Park, Berkeley, and we all hiked four to five miles—a way to demonstrate that regular exercise speeds recovery. Then we all ate breakfast at a restaurant together, which again provided a social milieu where nutritional discretion could be demonstrated and practiced. Many friendships developed in this close-knit atmosphere. Recovering people rediscovered how to relate socially without alcohol or other drugs. Their mutual support in sobriety became stronger than it might have been without the hikes, breakfasts, and dinners.

Prolonged alcohol and other drug use creates physical as well as emotional changes, which can inhibit free sexual functioning. Mickey and I discussed all sorts of sexual issues with our groups. Our participants had many doubts and many questions.

We explained that the varying degrees of physical and emotional sexuality changes which occur during alcohol/drug use are temporary and that, as health improves, these changes tend to slowly disappear. We told them that in our opinion by the end of the first year of recovery, 85 percent of alcohol/drug addicts spontaneously return to the sexual needs and practices that they had experienced prior to their addiction.

For those whose sexual problems persisted, we offered individual counseling twice weekly for a few weeks. Seldom did anyone in our groups require more prolonged and intense sex therapy.

In my experience, the propensity to develop close interpersonal relations returns slowly to recovering alcoholics/drug addicts. In my opinion, most need the physical release of sexual contact, although not all recovering persons require sex. Some may prefer celibacy, and we encouraged them accordingly.

Members of our groups practiced whatever sex they desired in their private lives. But we were careful to warn those who were not in committed relationships to be wary of attempting to establish new, deep, interpersonal commitments in the first year of recovery, perhaps becoming confused and thereby endangering their sobriety. Most recovering people are not ready for this kind of commitment in early sobriety.

Serious problems such as venereal diseases (today we would include AIDS, of course) were discussed openly and in detail, so that those who chose to engage in sexual relations could be clear about how to protect themselves. Those who chose celibacy received a useful sex education anyway.

In summary, in our professional groups we had frequent discussions about daily exercise, nutrition, the inherent toxicity in early recovery, the high prevalence of cross-addiction, the biogenetic nature of addiction, and sex. We offered opportunities, especially on weekends, to exercise together and to socialize at breakfast afterward. Group dinners after our evening meetings proved to be a sort of training center, in which socializing skills were relearned and practiced. These combined efforts brought group members closer together. This, in turn, enhanced their recoveries.

The span of attendance varied from six or eight months to several years. The groups are still going and include some of our original members.

Our success rate of individuals in these groups for maintaining sobriety was very high: over 90 percent for any given one-year period.

Alcoholics, other addicts, and AA

▲ ▲ ▲ ▲ ▲ ▲ ▲ ▲ ▲

I've heard some AA members say that in their opinions, addicts other than alcoholics should not be included in AA groups. They believe that the historic distinction between people addicted to alcohol and people addicted to other drugs should determine who is qualified to join AA.

Mickey and I were able to prove for ourselves, through our professional groups program, that both alcoholics and drug addicts can be treated successfully in the same group, using the same therapeutic techniques. We discovered that group support, coupled with AA principles, yielded excellent results. We found one major no-ticeable difference: in our groups, alcoholics usually recovered more slowly than did addicts to other drugs. The latter seemed to recover rather promptly, both physically and emotionally.

We felt great satisfaction in demonstrating that alcoholics and drug addicts can be treated together quite successfully, a practice that is now taking place in many inpatient and outpatient programs throughout the country. In my opinion, the AA Program can apply to both alcoholics and other drug addicts—and does, in many areas. Perhaps one day the bulk of AA members will agree.

MERRITT PERALTA INSTITUTE

In 1979-1980, Barbara Stern—a close friend of Mickey's and mine—combined two hospital chemical dependency treatment programs, Merritt and Peralta, into one free-standing chemical dependency unit which she directs: the Merritt Peralta Institute (MPI) in Oakland, California.

As in some other pioneer programs around the country, recovering alcoholics and drug addicts were housed and treated in the same facility, and the same treatment modalities were used for both. MPI has two full-time medical consultants: David E. Smith, M.D., MPI's director of research, as well as founder of San Francisco's Haight Ashbury Free Medical Clinic and a nationally known expert on chemical dependency, and Donald R. Wesson, M.D., who researched the use of naltrexone by opiate addicts for the maintenance of sobriety. MPI treats chemical addictions of all types as *primary* diseases. Barbara and her co-workers recognize the value of nutrition, exercise, sexual education, and family issues in recovery. In addition, MPI developed one of the first inpatient programs for family members in California.

Mickey and I were invited to lecture inpatients at MPI. She spoke on human sexuality issues for men and women, and on co-dependency problems. I lectured on the role of sex in recovery (stressing physiology), the biogenetic cause of alcohol/drug addiction, the high prevalence of cross-addiction, and the value of nutrition and exercise in recovery. Later Mickey worked as a chemical dependency counselor at MPI. We both felt very much a part of the Merritt Peralta Institute family.

An inpatient treatment center can work hand in hand with Alcoholics Anonymous and Narcotics Anonymous by creating a milieu for recovery from addiction smoothly and with safety. Some AA members that I've met resent treatment centers, saying that they infringe on the activities of Alcoholics Anonymous, and that only AA should be used by a recovering individual. This belief may stem from limited knowledge of the success of many treatment programs based on the Steps and principles of AA, as well as of the possible medical dangers of alcohol/drug toxicity in recovery. Dangers such as delirium tremens and convulsions decrease materially when patients are closely monitored medically and when medications are judiciously used during withdrawal. Appropriate monitoring of this sort can best be provided in qualified treatment facilities.

MELLOWING-OUT TIME IN DOBBINS

After several years in Oakland, I could see that I had slowly but persistently traveled through the four I's of Recovery, as described to me by George H. over three decades before. Coupled with that was a growing desire to retire. My final surgical case had been in Louisville on November 29, 1979. Since then, my practice of medicine had been limited to counseling chemically dependent people and their families. I was still active in AA, but less so. My urge to give AA talks was on the decline. My Blackboard Talk had changed as new scientific discoveries concerning addiction emerged; I presented my *new* Blackboard Talk from time to time, but less often than in the old days.

I noticed that if I described my turmoils as well as my joys at AA meetings, audience response to my trials was mixed. Some of the "I am right" boys still seem to me to linger under the delusion that after a few years in AA, life should be consistently beautiful. Some of them claim that I have not really grasped the AA Program. In my opinion, this is utter nonsense! *Of course* life is beautiful, but nevertheless, for me, sometimes the going gets rough. If an AA member doesn't like that and doesn't want to hear about it from me, too bad! A great surprise awaits him or her!

Since living in Saigon, I had simmered down, mellowed, and enjoyed an evolving sweetness in living. Now I felt that I'd become aware of the true nature of Alcoholics Anonymous: we are all alcoholics with different stories, who come to view life differently; we tackle our own problems in our own fashion; yet, at bottom, we are a unit of loving people. I am still irritable at times, still have my troubles and turmoils—but life is more beautiful than I could ever have imagined. Thank goodness for Mickey at this stage of my life. We work together, play together, yearn together, argue together, and love together. What could be more beautiful?

The urge to retire from addictions counseling grew strong. In 1984, with the professional groups' permissions, we passed the reins to Lyman B., a surgeon who had recovered beautifully from alcoholism. After he had been a trial leader for several months, and when it became apparent that he was ideal for the job, Mickey and I bowed out.

After that, I spent most of my time enjoying the facilities of the Oakland Athletic Club. Mickey took a short-term position as a chemical dependency counselor at Merritt Peralta Institute. Occasionally I counseled a private patient, but in the main I had retired from the active practice of medicine.

In June of 1984 I spoke at the first Unity Day AA meeting in the Marysville–Yuba City area about 130 miles northeast of San Francisco. We stayed a couple of nights with Rusty and Allison W. in their Marysville home. Mickey noticed how reasonable real estate prices were in this area compared with San Francisco. Just for fun, we called a local realtor. I told him that I had once lived at Lake Tahoe and liked it very much.

"I have a very nice property in the Sierra Nevada foothills about thirty miles northeast of here," the realtor said. "It's very rustic and unique." The next day, when his partner took us to see the house in Dobbins, it was love at first sight. The price was reasonable and affordable. Impulsively, we bought it. Two months later we left Oakland for Dobbins.

Dobbins' surroundings are quiet, rustic, and lovely. We already knew Marve H., an energetic AA member who lives in Dobbins and had been sober for about a year when we moved there. Her husband, Rich, had sobered up by himself about twelve years before, but with Marve's involvement in the Program, he became interested as well. We joined the small Dobbins AA group, which Marve had started shortly before we arrived. We attended every week, and now the group has grown considerably and is going strong.

Dobbins is a typically rural, small community, with a post office, two tiny grocery stores, and little else—except magnificant surroundings. Small homes are sprinkled throughout the Sierra Nevada foothills. There are no distinct boundaries, and there is a sense of being a small, closely knit community. We made new friends, both young and old, and we attended our small AA meeting every Wednesday evening at seven-thirty at the Lake Francis Grange Hall in the village.

One delightful new AA experience during my Dobbins sojourn was joining the "Coffee Cup Campers." This group was started by "GI Bob" C., who had sobered up about three decades before while in the U.S. Air Force in North Africa, then lived for many years in the Carolinas, where there was a Coffee Cup Camper group. Our northern California group numbered about fifty AA members and their families (including half a dozen children), who met at the Hornswoggle Camp Grounds just north of Dobbins the first weekend of each month, April through September. RV's, motor homes, tent trailers, tents, and other rigs jammed the area. No electricity, but water was available. Mickey and I had a six-by-ten-foot tent trailer. Activities included fishing, hiking, swimming, AA talk, and a small penny ante card game that attracted a large crowd. Each evening we held an open AA meeting around a campfire. The wide open spaces in the California mountains offered a great opportunity for AA members to meet in a very natural setting. I found my love for AA strengthened in the woods: each tree was part of a great forest, just as each AA member is part of a great Fellowship.

Another treat in Dobbins was seeing Jack E. again.

Jack had been a member of our Saigon AA group. He'd spent several years in Saudi Arabia and other parts of the Middle East. One day in Saigon he told me, "I'm confused and bewildered, and people tell me I'm too irascible and restless. What can I do?"

I said with a smile, "You're sober. So why *not* be confused, irascible and restless—if that's your nature!"

Jack later told me that he found that remark enormously comforting. "It seemed all right to be myself."

Jack and I left Saigon in 1974. I traveled to India via Singapore and he to the Middle East via Hong Kong. I lost track of him.

Years later, when Mickey and I were living in Dobbins, by one of those chance crisscrossing of paths that seem to happen frequently in AA, Jack showed up at our Wednesday evening Dobbins meeting. We had a great reunion!

Jack was living in a small town about fifty miles away with his Vietnamese wife and his daughter. Jack is a devoted AA member. We visit each other's meetings from time to time and discuss Saigon days.

Jack says he is *still* confused, irascible, and restless, but the rest of us in AA appreciate his good humor and maturity. Obviously, he has learned to accept himself.

In Dobbins the residue of my turmoil receded. In general, life was leisurely and relaxed. We had a lovely home, walked miles every day with our dog, and afterwards enjoyed our outdoor sauna and hot spa. From time to time, we saw a counseling patient or two. Mickey kept a very productive garden. On summer evenings we sat out on the deck and watched the sun set. In winter, we cuddled up by the wood stove and petted the cat.

We had left the fast lane of living.

Control, power, and a God of my understanding

▲ ▲ ▲ ▲ ▲ ▲ ▲ ▲ ▲

Newcomers to AA may oscillate between denying their addiction on the one hand, and mourning their loss of control over alcohol/drugs on the other.

As a newcomer, I remember feeling deeply lost and bewildered. I cried out in anguish, If I can't have control and if I am powerless, then who and what does have control? Who and what is powerful?

At this point, the first glimmer of a Power greater than myself was born. This spiritual recognition was the keystone of my sobriety in AA. By giving up, I had gained! I came to see that sobriety had a power of its own.

Later in my recovery, when I confronted individuals and situations in and out of AA that irritated me, I said to myself, I may be powerless over alcohol and other drugs, but I am not powerless over that individual or that situation. Then I realized I had grabbed back some of my denial and control.

When I embraced powerlessness and lack of control over the use of alcohol and drugs, I expe-

rienced the joy of growing sobriety. AA's Second Step ("Came to believe that a Power greater than ourselves could restore us to sanity") became part of a natural sequence of events. *I* can't control my using or drinking, but a Power greater than myself *can*! Once I accepted this Step, it naturally led to the Third Step. And then I said, not only am I powerless over drugs and alcohol, I can see that I am really powerless over *all* aspects of my life. I must do the legwork and live it, but the impetus to do so must come from a Higher Power.

I believed that there was no way I could *decide* to turn my will and life over to the care of God, as we understand Him. After all, the entity that *demands* the turning over is the *ego*, and my ego is the trouble! Before long I came to rely on the Second Step simply happening. Joyfully, I left the control to my own personalized concept of God. Without realizing it, I had taken the Third Step.

The first three Steps tumble one into the other, and lead to the personal housecleaning in Steps Four through Nine. I learned that by discussing my problems with someone, by standing ready to have a Higher Power regulate my life, and by making amends to those whom I had hurt, my sobriety could grow into a happy state.

The longer I am sober and clean, the more my denial fades. With the joys of powerlessness and loss of control that I have found in sobriety, I can relax and watch my life unfold.

I cannot help but be very grateful that I am alcoholic. After all, without alcohol and other drugs, I might not have crashed to the bottom, lost control, recognized powerlessness, and experienced this joy in sobriety.

Some years ago, Al G. overheard his AA sponsor, Frank P., say, "Your life is none of your business." Al added, "The only thing you have to do is 'hang out' and watch it all happen—and live it."

These statements are a way of rephrasing the Third Step of AA, "Made a decision to turn our will and our lives over to the care of God as we understood Him." If my life is "turned over," my life is no longer my own business.

When I clearly recognized that I was an alcoholic and then discovered and relied on a Power greater than myself, sobriety followed. To this day, my sobriety depends on an inner confidence that my life is in the hands of a God of my understanding.

THE OLD-TIMERS FORUM

"Old-timer: a veteran; an oldster."

American Heritage Dictionary, Second College Edition

After about eight years in AA, some members disappear and never return. This does not necessarily mean that they drink again. It does mean that their AA meetings no longer appeal to them, and they stop coming.

I organized an "Old-Timers Forum" at the Hub Alano Club in Marysville, California (near Dobbins), for discussion about any issues pertinent to long-term sobriety. But any AA or NA member—newcomer or old-timer—along with his or her family, was welcome. Probably due to this open-door policy, after about eight months we changed the group's name to "Friday Night Forum" because our newcomers said that they didn't want old-timers telling them how to stay sober!

Old-timers who came to the Old-Timers Forum brought up the following complaints about AA:

▲ They were *bored by drunkalogues.* Some said that they were bored at certain AA meetings because they "heard nothing but drunkalogues"—detailed reminiscences of drunken behavior—including their own. Our drinking histories are only part of AA sharing: we need to share many other issues at closed meetings.

▲ They were *bored with emphasis on early sobriety.* Other old-timers said some AA groups did "nothing but discuss early sobriety," which they found boring. If it's a beginners' meeting, then early sobriety will be the focus, and these old-timers might be more comfortable finding a meeting that is not intended for beginners.

▲They were *irritated by emphasis on physical recovery*. Others found that stressing *only* physical recovery at AA meetings was too limiting.

▲They were sometimes *reluctant to share*. Instead of voicing their inner doubts and dissatisfactions about AA meetings, some left AA—from boredom, or fear that they might upset newcomers. Failing to share with other AA members usually hurts the silent ones the most.

▲They sometimes *reacted to arrogant newer members*. Roberta, an old-timer sober for twenty-three years, told me that she had decided to attend only an occasional meeting because some far newer members (with three, four, and five years of sobriety) wanted to tell her how to stay sober—instead of focusing on how they themselves stayed sober. Annoyed, she told them, "Wait until *you've* been sober for twenty-three years, and then you can tell me how I should work the Program." This kind of conflict can be avoided if all AA members remain aware that in AA meetings we "*share* our experience, strength, and hope with each other," and "place principles before personalities."

▲They sometimes *objected to those who were polyaddicted*. Paul G., another old-timer, wrote me the following note: "What's this I hear that you are all for admitting cocaine-, heroin-, and pot-users into full AA membership? I hope you are not!"

I certainly don't mind attending an AA meeting which includes members addicted to drugs other than alcohol. Nonetheless, our experience at our Old-Timers Forum was that a good number of old-timers have left AA because of discomfort with the new, polyaddicted member. This is sad, because AA groups are changing. Today, in my area of California, polyaddicted AA members are in the majority. "Pure alcoholics" are in the minority. In my opinion, we all need to join hands and sit together in AA groups.

The 1986 AA demographic survey, conducted by AA's General Service Office and designed to indicate current trends in membership characteristics, showed that 38 percent in the AA Program are "addicted to a drug (in addition to their alcoholism)." This "strong increase" follows an upward trend: the 1980 AA survey showed 24 percent; the 1983 survey showed 31 percent.

> ▲*AA has become a low priority in their lives.* Some old-timers have left AA (or attend meetings infrequently) because their lives have expanded and their interests are elsewhere. They no longer feel that their sobriety depends on constant AA attendance. Some of these old-timers tell us that even though they believe that their sobriety is solid, they feel a sense of incompletion.

I still go to AA meetings at least two to three times a week simply because I *like* AA meetings and AA people!

The 'I have arrived' fallacy

▲ ▲ ▲ ▲ ▲ ▲ ▲ ▲ ▲

Sometimes I feel that because of my long-term sobriety, I must appear wise and "know-it-all." This can give me the feeling of being a fraud—particularly if I fall for the fallacy that "I have arrived," therefore my emotional troubles should vanish. Actually, the quality of my sobriety is threatened by this type of thinking. Tears, anger, resentment, and a sense of alienation from others can become recurrent; suffering and loneliness return.

Despite my long-term sobriety, I sometimes harbor unforgiving attitudes towards others. These feelings knock the sweetness of my long-term sobriety into a cocked hat! I am sometimes restless. I may yearn for something new and exciting to happen. But I have learned to accept the unrest and thereby to love the current instant for what it is. All too frequently I forget that.

In sobriety, especially in long-term sobriety, one can be tossed between serenity and misery. And this old-timer can succumb to the notion that my misery is inappropriate. The demand to be a perfect old-timer and to be perfectly serene can be haunting.

For me, the bottom line in AA is: pay attention to sobriety, and good things are bound to happen.

Back to the San Francisco Bay Area!

"Life to me is a combination of greatness, ecstasy, awfulness, painful awareness, bewildering blindness, and, at times, awesome clarity. The whole thing is too gloriously wonderful and awful to seek simple and lasting answers. Temporary answers, yes, but not lasting ones. The temporary answers that come through working the AA program are, to me, breathers until the next dark and glorious episode. Though I struggle, and at times hate it, I would have it no other way."

E.M.M., "Life!," *AA Grapevine*, June 1966

In the winter of 1987 I developed intense right knee pain when walking, which persisted for six weeks. I had always been an avid walker, covering three or more miles per day. I consulted an orthopedist friend in the San Francisco area. He reported that I had worn out the cartilage in my right knee and needed a total knee replacement. From now on, hiking in mountainous terrain would be unwise.

With great reluctance, Mickey and I decided we had to leave Dobbins. Our mountain retreat there had been refreshing and nourishing, but in September 1987 we moved to Walnut Creek, a community in the San Francisco Bay area.

In October of that year I had a total right knee replacement operation. My recovery has been excellent. I'm as good as new—back walking and exercising!

Mickey returned to work at the Merritt Peralta Institute. I became a consultant to Parkside Recovery Center's Outpatient Chemical Dependency Unit in San Ramon, about ten miles from

our home, offering a series of once-a-week lectures to patients and
their families on:

1. the biogenetic aspects of addiction,

2. the physical and emotional consequences of addiction to
   specific substances—alcohol, cocaine, amphetamines, other
   "uppers" and "downers"—with video tapes as adjuncts,

3. exercise and nutrition in recovery,

4. the sexual aspects of recovery,

5. the anatomy of emotional change in recovery.

The group discussions that follow the lectures are usually very
lively.

I also started a Family Forum, which includes alcoholics and
addicts of all types and their families. We meet once a week in
Walnut Creek. The format encourages open and free discussion
with a lot of feedback between members. This is not strictly an AA
meeting; all members attend AA or NA as well. The purpose of the
Family Forum is to combine support therapy with AA principles,
in order to avoid a relapse and a return to drinking or using. We
strive to pinpoint early symptoms which could lead to a relapse and
bring them into the open, so that changes and/or additions to each
person's program can be instituted to ensure a lasting sobriety.
Proper nutrition and a daily exercise regime are strongly emphasized.

I have learned that retirement does not mean stopping. It
simply means changing direction with a new energy and a new point
of view—and, in my case, AA is the center of it all.

I don't "practice" the AA Program these days (although others
would probably say I do). I like to believe that I review it daily and
new meanings *dawn* on me. The Program leads me to new interpretations. After thirty-five years in the Program, I still use the
books *Alcoholics Anonymous* and *Twelve Steps and Twelve Traditions*
to foster new ideas about my sobriety and living. Long ago I

memorized Chapter Five and many other parts of the Big Book, and the Twelve Steps, and the Twelve Traditions. To this day, I still repeat them to myself. They have served me well every day of my sober life.

Spiritual awakening and miracles

▲ ▲ ▲ ▲ ▲ ▲ ▲ ▲ ▲

For us alcoholics and other drug addicts, spiritual life *begins* when recovery begins. In some individuals, the spiritual awakening referred to in Step Twelve resembles a "hot flash" of immense proportions. In others, the spiritual awakening occurs in tiny increments, barely perceptible emotional mutations.

The important thing to me is that spiritual awareness and growth occur constantly during my recovery, no matter how small the experience. Many of us eagerly anticipate a magical upheaval, a "spiritual change." In my opinion, a great "hot flash" is not necessary. Spirituality is inherent in each tiny, seemingly ordinary step of physical and emotional recovery. For example, a person's change from be-ing an active to a sober drunk is a miracle! But because it is now so commonplace in the AA Program, many discount these small steps as spiritual experiences.

When we slowly and painfully share our experience, strength, and hope with one another, we draw closer together and a magical thing does, indeed, happen! Sobriety becomes important, and drinking and using incidental. No physician, no psychologist, no other medical/scientific expert can explain why. It is beyond rationale. We undergo a change. We become different. The great magic is that recovery is ours. In fact, we ourselves are the miracle!

The Twelve Steps of AA

STEP ONE
"We admitted we were powerless over alcohol—that our lives had become unmanageable."

STEP TWO
"Came to believe that a Power greater than ourselves could restore us to sanity."

STEP THREE
"Made a decision to turn our will and our lives over to the care of God as we understood Him."

STEP FOUR
"Made a searching and fearless moral inventory of ourselves."

STEP FIVE
"Admitted to God, to ourselves, and to another human being the exact nature of our wrongs."

STEP SIX
"Were entirely ready to have God remove all these defects of character."

STEP SEVEN
"Humbly asked Him to remove our shortcomings."

STEP EIGHT
"Made a list of all persons we had harmed, and became willing to make amends to them all."

STEP NINE
"Made direct amends to such people wherever possible, except when to do so would injure them or others."

STEP TEN
"Continued to take personal inventory and when we were wrong promptly admitted it."

STEP ELEVEN
"Sought through prayer and meditation to improve our conscious contact with God as we understood Him, praying only for knowledge of His will for us and the power to carry that out."

STEP TWELVE
"Having had a spiritual awakening as the result of these Steps, we tried to carry this message to alcoholics, and to practice these principles in all our affairs."

The Twelve Traditions of AA

TRADITION ONE
"Our common welfare should come first; personal recovery depends upon AA unity."

TRADITION TWO
"For our group purpose there is but one ultimate authority—a loving God as He may express Himself in our group conscience. Our leaders are but trusted servants; they do not govern."

TRADITION THREE
"The only requirement for AA membership is a desire to stop drinking."

TRADITION FOUR
"Each group should be autonomous except in matters affecting other groups or AA as a whole."

TRADITION FIVE
"Each group has but one primary purpose—to carry its message to the alcoholic who still suffers."

TRADITION SIX
"An AA group ought never endorse, finance, or lend the AA name to any related facility or outside enterprise, lest problems of money, property, and prestige divert us from our primary purpose."

TRADITION SEVEN
"Every AA group ought to be fully self-supporting, declining outside contributions."

TRADITION EIGHT
"Alcoholics Anonymous should remain forever nonprofessional, but our service centers may employ special workers."

TRADITION NINE
"AA, as such, ought never be organized; but we may create service boards or committees directly responsible to those they serve."

TRADITION TEN
Alcoholics Anonymous has no opinion on outside issues; hence the AA name ought never be drawn into public controversy.

TRADITION ELEVEN
"Our public relations policy is based on attraction rather than promotion; we need always maintain personal anonymity at the level of press, radio, and films."

TRADITION TWELVE
"Anonymity is the spiritual foundation of all our traditions, ever reminding us to place principles before personalities."

The Twelve Steps and Twelve Traditions are reprinted with permission of Alcoholics Anonymous World Services, Inc.

Thoughts on Addiction

The following are "myths" and "realities" about alcoholism, taken from the James R. Milam - Katherine Ketcham book *Under the Influence.* Mickey and I agree with Dr. Milam on all these points, with our added comments in parentheses.

Although these statements focus expressly on alcohol addiction, in our opinion they are equally applicable to all addictive drugs, (e.g., sedatives, hypnotics, opiates, amphetamines, cocaine, etc.) with some minor differences, depending on the drug.

Myth: Alcohol is predominantly a sedative or depressant drug.

Reality: Alcohol's pharmacological effects change with the amount drunk. In small quantities, alcohol is a stimulant. In large quantities, alcohol acts as a sedative. In all amounts, however, alcohol provides a rich and potent source of calories and energy.

Myth: Alcohol has the same chemical and physiological effect on everyone who drinks.

Reality: Alcohol, like every other food we take into our bodies, affects different people in different ways.

Myth: Alcohol is an addictive drug, and anyone who drinks long and hard enough will become addicted.

Reality: Alcohol is a selectively addictive drug; it is addictive for only a minority of its users, namely, alcoholics. Most people can drink occasionally, daily, even heavily, without becoming addicted to alcohol.

Others (alcoholics) will become addicted no matter how much they drink (some 10 to 15 percent of Americans who drink).

Myth: Addiction to alcohol is often psychological.

Reality: Addiction to alcohol is primarily physiological. Alcoholics become addicted because their bodies are physiologically incapable of processing alcohol normally.

Myth: People become alcoholics because they have psychological or emotional problems which they try to relieve by drinking.

Reality: Alcoholics have the same psychological and emotional problems as everyone else before they start drinking. These problems are aggravated by their addiction to alcohol. Alcoholism undermines and weakens the alcoholic's ability to cope with the normal problems of living. Furthermore, the alcoholic's emotions become inflamed both when he drinks excessively and when he stops drinking. Thus, when he is drinking and when he is abstinent, he will feel angry, fearful, and depressed to exaggerated degrees.

(A growing number of scientists no longer believe in the psychological causation theory of addiction to alcohol or other drugs. Some addicts believe that they are psychological cripples because early life experiences created their addiction. These addicts can suffer deep guilt, doubt, and disablingly low self-esteem. Modern observations of the biogenetic, inherited cause of addiction say that addiction is a primary disease in itself—not secondary to assumed psychological problems.

Many nonaddicts use drugs [alcohol, sedatives, cocaine, amphetamines, and the like] in order to decrease stress. In the beginning, addicts use drugs [including alcohol] for the same purpose. However, because of the addicts' inherited biological and physiological makeup, they react differently and in the course of time develop an addiction to their drug of choice. The nonaddict counterparts do not. Over time, as a result of using mood-changing drugs of any sort, addicts become isolated. Their personalities fail to grow because their interpersonal relations are scattered and fractured. They then develop psychological and emotional problems, which are not the cause but the result of isolation and of drinking alcohol and/or using other drugs.)

Myth: When the alcoholic is drinking, he reveals his true personality.

Reality: Alcohol's effect on the brain causes severe psychological and emotional distortions of the normal personality. Sobriety reveals the alcoholic's true personality.

Myth: All sorts of social problems—marriage problems, a death in the family, job stress—may cause alcoholism.

Reality: As with psychological and emotional problems, alcoholics experience all the social pressures everyone else does, but their ability to cope is undermined by the disease and the problems get worse.

(Social problems often trigger drinking in both alcoholics and nonalcoholics, but it is the alcohol itself, in a susceptible person that triggers alcoholism, not the reasons for drinking it.)

Myth: The fact that alcoholics often continue to be depressed, anxious, irritable, and unhappy after they stop drinking is evidence that their disease is caused by psychological problems.

Reality: Alcoholics who continue to be depressed, anxious, irritable, and unhappy after they stop drinking are actually suffering from a phenomenon called "the protracted withdrawal syndrome." The physical damage caused by years of excessive drinking has not been completely reversed; they are, in fact, still sick and in need of more effective therapy.

Myth: If people would only drink responsibly they would not become alcoholics.

Reality: Many responsible drinkers become alcoholics. Then, because it is the nature of the disease {not the person}, they begin to drink irresponsibly.

Myth: An alcoholic has to want help to be helped.

(This was the premise when AA was founded: that an alcoholic had to "hit bottom" before AA would be effective.)

Reality: Most drinking alcoholics do not want to be helped. They are sick, unable to think rationally, and incapable of giving up alcohol by themselves. Most recovered alcoholics were forced into treatment against their will. Self-motivation usually occurs during treatment, not before.

Myth: Some alcoholics can learn to drink normally and can continue to drink with no ill effects as long as they limit the amount.

Reality: Alcoholics can never safely return to drinking because drinking in any amount will sooner or later reactivate their addiction.

(If there are exceptions, they are rare and no one knows how to ascertain who they are.)

Myth: Psychotherapy can help many alcoholics achieve sobriety through self-understanding.

Reality: Psychotherapy diverts attention from the physical cause of the disease, compounds the alcoholic's guilt and shame, and aggravates rather than alleviates his problems.

(There is little or no useful psychotherapeutic self-understanding while the alcoholic still drinks.)

Myth: Craving for alcohol can be offset by eating high-sugar foods.

Reality: Foods with a high sugar content will increase the alcoholic's depression, irritability, and tension and intensify his desire for a drink to relieve these symptoms.

Myth: If alcoholics eat three balanced meals a day, their nutritional problems will eventually correct themselves.

Reality: Alcoholics' nutritional needs are only partially met by a balanced diet. They also need vitamin and mineral supplements to correct any deficiencies and to maintain nutritional balances.

Myth: Tranquilizers and sedatives are sometimes useful in treating alcoholics.

Reality: Tranquilizers and sedatives are useful only during the acute withdrawal period! Beyond that, these substitute drugs are destructive and, in many cases, deadly for alcoholics.

(Many of these substitute drugs are just as addictive as alcohol.)

Resources

Alcoholics Anonymous

The AA Service Manual. New York: AA World Services, 1969.

✔ *Alcoholics Anonymous* ("Big Book"). 3rd ed. New York: AA World Services, 1939, 1976.

Alcoholics Anonymous Comes of Age. New York: AA World Services, 1955.

A Member's Eye View of Alcoholics Anonymous (pamphlet). New York: AA World Services, 1970.

✔ *As Bill Sees It.* New York: AA World Services, 1967.

✔ *Came to Believe...* New York: AA World Services, 1973.

The Co-Founders of Alcoholics Anonymous (pamphlet). New York: AA World Services, 1972, 1975.

Dr. Bob and the Good Old Timers. New York: AA World Services, 1980.

44 Questions (pamphlet). New York: AA World Services, 1952, rev. 1978.

✔ *Living Sober.* New York: AA World Services, 1975.

✔ *Pass It On—The Story of Bill Wilson and How the AA Message Reached the World.* New York: AA World Services, 1984.

✔ *Twelve Steps and Twelve Traditions.* New York: AA World Services, 1952, 1953.

All AA literature can be purchased through local Alcoholics Anonymous offices, or ordered from the General Service Office of AA, Box 459, Grand Central Station, New York, NY 10163.

Al-Anon

Al-Anon Faces Alcoholism. New York: Al-Anon Family Group Headquarters, 1965, 1981.

Al-Anon Family Groups. New York: Al-Anon Family Group Headquarters, 1966, 1981.

Al-Anon's Twelve Steps and Twelve Traditions. New York: Al-Anon Family Group Headquarters, 1981.

The Dilemma of the Alcoholic Marriage. New York: Al-Anon Family Group Headquarters, 1971.

Is There An Alcoholic in Your Life? New York: Al-Anon Family Group Headquarters.

One Day at a Time in Al-Anon. New York: Al-Anon Family Group Headquarters, 1986.

All Al-Anon literature can be purchased through local Al-Anon offices or ordered from Al-Anon Family Group Headquarters, Inc., P.O. Box 862, Midtown Station, New York, NY 10018-0862.

AA Grapevine

The Best of the Grapevine. New York: The AA Grapevine Inc. 1985.

"The Whisper of Humility," *AA Grapevine,* March 1955: 2-5. Reprinted November 1956, November 1964, November 1977.

"Here's Why," *AA Grapevine,* April 1959: 13-18.

"To Finland with Love," *AA Grapevine,* December 1965: 7-10.

"Thank God for Despair," *AA Grapevine,* June 1965: 12.

"Search for Cloud Nine," *AA Grapevine,* April 1977: 33-36.

"Our Greatest Safeguard," *AA Grapevine,* May 1979: 34-35.

"Life!" *AA Grapevine,* June 1966: 43.

AA Grapevine literature is available from the AA Grapevine, Inc., P.O. Box 1980, Grand Central Station, New York, NY 10163.

Narcotics Anonymous

Narcotics Anonymous. *Narcotics Anonymous.* Sun Valley, Calif.: C.A.R.E.N.A. Publishing, 1982. (Box 622, Sun Valley, CA 91352.)

All NA literature can be purchased through local Narcotics Anonymous offices or ordered from World Service Office, Inc., Narcotics Anonymous, 16155 Wyandotte Street, Van Nuys, CA 91406.

Other Sources

Anderson, Bob. *Stretching.* Bolinas, Calif.: Shelter Publications, Inc., 1980.

Bailey, Covert. *Fit or Fat.* Boston: Houghton, Mifflin, 1978.

Bissell, LeClair, M.D., and Paul W. Haberman. *Alcoholism in the Professions.* New York: Oxford University Press, 1984.

Blum, Kenneth, Ph.D. *Handbook of Usable Drugs.* New York: Gardner Press, 1984.

Chuck C. *A New Pair of Glasses.* Irvine, Calif.: New-Look Publishing, 1984.

Fixx, James. *The Complete Book of Running.* New York: Random House, 1978.

Ford, Betty, with Chris Chase. *The Times of My Life.* New York: Ballantine Books, 1979.

Gitlow, Stanley E., M.D., and Herbert S. Peyser, M.D., eds. *Alcoholism: A Practical Treatment Guide.* New York: Grune and Stratton, 1980.

Goodwin, Donald, M.D. *Is Alcoholism Hereditary?* New York: Oxford University Press, 1976.

Haight Ashbury Publications. "Sexological Aspects of Substance Use and Abuse" in *Journal of Psychoactive Drugs.* 14(1-2). San Francisco: January-June 1982.

Haworth Press. *Advances in Alcohol and Substance Abuse,* part of a series. New York: Haworth Press. (Request listing from Haworth Press, 28 East 22nd Street, New York, NY 10010.)

Jellinek, E.M. *The Disease Concept of Alcoholism.* New Haven, Conn.: Hillhouse Press, 1960.

Johnson, Vernon E. *I'll Quit Tomorrow*. New York: Harper and Row, 1973.

Keller, Mark, Mairi McCormick, and Vera Efron. *A Dictionary of Words about Alcohol*. 2nd ed., New Brunswick, N.J.: Rutgers Center of Alcohol Studies, 1968, 1982.

Ketcham, Katherine, and L. Ann Mueller, M.D. *Eating Right to Live Sober*. Seattle: Madrona Publishers, 1983.

Kinsey, Alfred C., Wardell B. Pomeroy, and Clyde E. Martin. *Sexual Behavior in the Human Male*. Philadelphia: W. B. Saunders, 1948.

Kinsey, Alfred C., Wardell B. Pomeroy, Clyde E. Martin, and Paul H. Gebhard. *Sexual Behavior in the Human Female*. Philadelphia: W. B. Saunders, 1953.

Krishnamurti, J. *The Only Revolution*. Ojai, Calif.: Krishnamurti Foundation. (This and other books by Krishnamurti can be obtained from the Krishnamurti Foundation, Box 216, Ojai, CA 93023.)

Lappe, Frances Moore. *Diet for a Small Planet*. New York: Ballantine Books, 1975.

Lieber, Charles S., M.D. *Metabolic Aspects of Alcoholism*. Lancaster, England: MTP Press, 1977.

Lieber, Charles S., M.D., and Barry Stimmel, M.D., eds. *Recent Advances in the Biology of Alcoholism*. New York: Haworth Press, 1982.

Mann, Marty. *Marty Mann Answers Your Questions about Drinking and Alcoholism*. New York: Holt, Rinehart and Winston, 1970.

————. *New Primer on Alcoholism*. New York: Holt, Rinehart and Winston.

Masters, William H., and Virginia E. Johnson. *Human Sexual Response*. Boston: Little, Brown, 1966.

Maxwell, Ruth. *The Booze Battle*. New York: Ballantine Books, 1976.

Milam, James R., Ph.D., and Katherine Ketcham. *Under the Influence*. Seattle: Madrona Publishers, 1981.

Mueller, L. Ann, M.D., and Katherine Ketcham. *Recovering. How to Get and Stay Sober*. New York: Bantam Books, 1987.

Paul H. *Things My Sponsor Taught Me*. Center City, Minn.: Hazelden, 1987.

Pomeroy, Wardell B. *Dr. Kinsey and the Institute for Sex Research.* New York: Harper and Row, 1972.

Robe, Lucy Barry. *Co-Starring Famous Women and Alcohol.* Minneapolis: CompCare Publishers, 1986.

Robe, Lucy Barry. *Just So It's Healthy—Drinking and Drugs Can Harm Your Unborn Baby.* Rev. ed. Minneapolis: CompCare Publishers, 1982.

Robertson, Laurel. *Laurel's Kitchen.* Petaluma, Calif.: Nilgiri Press, 1976.

Robertson, Laurel. *The New Laurel's Kitchen.* 2nd ed. Berkeley, Calif.: Ten Speed Press, 1986.

Schuckit, Marc, M.D. "Alcoholism and Genetics: Possible Biological Markers," *Biological Psychiatry* 15(3), 437-447.

Schwartz, Leonard. *Heavy Hands.* Boston: Little, Brown, 1982.

Talbott, G. Douglas, and Margaret Cooney, G.N.S.H. *Today's Disease.* Springfield, Ill.: Charles C. Thomas, 1982.

World Book Encyclopedia. Chicago: World Book, 1984.